Goldwin Smith, Henry Longueville Mansel

Rational Religion and the Rationalistic Objections of the Bampton

Lectures for 1858

Goldwin Smith, Henry Longueville Mansel

Rational Religion and the Rationalistic Objections of the Bampton Lectures for 1858

ISBN/EAN: 9783743441675

Manufactured in Europe, USA, Canada, Australia, Japa

Cover: Foto ©Lupo / pixelio.de

Manufactured and distributed by brebook publishing software (www.brebook.com)

Goldwin Smith, Henry Longueville Mansel

Rational Religion and the Rationalistic Objections of the Bampton

Lectures for 1858

RATIONAL RELIGION,

AND THE

RATIONALISTIC OBJECTIONS

OF THE

BAMPTON LECTURES FOR 1858.

BY

GOLDWIN SMITH.

———

"It is of little importance by what authority an opinion is sanctioned, if it will not itself stand the test of sound criticism."—*Preface to the Third Edition of Mr. Mansel's Bampton Lectures.*

———

OXFORD:
J. L. WHEELER.
WHITTAKER & CO., LONDON.
1861.

PREFACE.

In one of my lectures on the Study of History, when I was searching for the true key to the History of Man, I introduced the following passage :—" The question then is, Can " we find any hypothesis in accordance with " the facts of history which will reconcile the " general course of history to our sense of " justice ? I say to our sense of justice. I " assume here that man has really been created " in the image of God ; that the morality of " man points true, however remotely, to the " morality of God ; that human justice is " identical with divine justice, and is therefore " a real key to the history of the world. ' If,' " says Clarke, ' justice and goodness be not " the same in God as in our ideas, then we " mean nothing when we say that God is " necessarily just and good ; and for the same " reason it may as well be said that we know " not what we mean, when we affirm that He " is an intelligent and wise Being ; and there " will be no foundation at all left on which " we can fix anything. Thus the *moral*

" *attributes* of God, however they may be " acknowledged in words, yet in reality they " are by these men entirely taken away ; and " upon the same grounds, the *natural attributes* " may also be denied. And so, upon the " whole, this opinion likewise, if we argue upon " it consistently, must finally recur to absolute " atheism.' Either to absolute atheism, or to " the belief in a God who is mere power, " and to religion which is mere submission " to power, without moral sympathy or " allegiance."

The doctrine that the Human Morality is identical with the Divine, and that the moral nature of man points truly, though remotely, to that of God, which is embodied in the words of Clarke above quoted, forms the basis of the philosophy of history adopted in my lectures. It also forms the basis of Rational Religion. It had been controverted with great ability by Mr. Mansel in his Bampton Lectures for 1858; and those lectures had been received with such general applause in the University, that the opposite doctrine advocated in them might be said to be, to a great extent, in possession of the field.

When I published my lecture, I appended a Postscript defending Clarke's doctrine of the identity of the Divine and Human Morality against the arguments of the Bampton Lectures, by showing that the opposite doctrine would lead us to the absurdity of atheism.

Mr. Mansel, after some interval, published a reply to this Postscript, in the form of a letter addressed to me, towards the end of last Term. There was not time to answer his letter before the commencement of the Long Vacation, more especially as he had appealed to books, the convenient use of which, though he seems to think the knowledge of them general among us, was not very easily obtained. But I circulated among the Academical community, of which we are both members, and to which we both owe the observance of social rules, a paper repudiating certain unmannerly accusations which he had, very gratuitously, as I hope and believe, put into my mouth. The substance of that paper is repeated in this Preface.

I now republish the Postscript to my Lectures with a defence of it against Mr. Mansel's Letter. I have thought it better to cast the defence into the same form with the original arguments than to cast it into the form of a letter addressed to Mr. Mansel.

I do not believe controversy to be an evil if it is conducted fairly, temperately, and with a determination to come to a decisive issue. I believe that it is the only mode we have of settling disputed questions. But this at least is certain, that when a controversy about an important question has once arisen, it is best, in the interest of peace as well as of truth, that it should be brought to a definite result. I am not without hope that some advantage may accrue to Oxford especially from a frank discussion of this matter; and that philosophy among us may begin henceforth to aspire to a nobler part than that of paralysing the reason of man at the moment when, between great hopes and great fears, he is making an earnest and anxious effort to find a way through his perplexities and arrive at religious truth. The experience of history proves that when reason is paralysed, man becomes the slave not of superstition only, but of sense.

I think it is as well to dispose in this preface of all matters not directly affecting the philosophical question, which forms the only important subject of discussion. Some charges of misrepresentation which Mr. Mansel has made against me, on account of certain passages in my Postscript, will be dealt with in notes to the passages to which they severally relate.

In the commencement of his letter to me,

Mr. Mansel obliquely raises a point of order on which I need not dwell long. I must regard the principle on which the philosophy of history adopted by me is based, and the defence of that principle against current objections, as falling not within "a different department of study," but within my own. A "scientific" philosophy of history necessarily sets out from a scientific principle. A religious philosophy of history as necessarily sets out from a theological principle. Theology and the religious philosophy of history thus border on each other, though their spheres are distinct. I feel no jealousy when a theologian touches, for his purposes, on the philosophy of history. I felt no jealousy when the Bampton Lecturer who succeeded Mr. Mansel laid down rules of historical evidence, though I should have ventured to suggest some modifications in the rules which he laid down. This, however, is a subject on which I will not trouble Mr. Mansel with prolix apologies, because it is one on which, having regard to the nature of the questions now raised touching the philosophy of history, and acting, as I hope, under a due sense of responsibility, I am prepared to form my own judgment and to take my own course.

I do not forget that I have the honor—I sincerely regard it as an honor—to number Mr. Mansel among my "brother professors." But the late Mr. Baden Powell, who was pretty sharply attacked in the notes to Mr. Mansel's first lecture, was one of the same brotherhood. So is Mr. Jowett, who was attacked less directly but perhaps not less injuriously in the same place, by the association of his name with those of Socinus, Priestley, Fichte, and other writers most odious to the Church.

From the point of order, Mr. Mansel passes to a warm defence of his own personal character, which it would be very wrong to impugn, and which, I trust, I have in no way impugned. The Edinburgh Review spoke of his book as "an attack on the Divine Morality"; an expression which was perhaps capable of misinterpretation, though I do not suppose it was actually misinterpreted: and this offence, of which I was entirely guiltless, is put in the front of a pamphlet purporting to be a reply to me. Mr. Mansel has been so good as to assure me, in answer to my expostulation, that he does not consider me responsible for any statement made in the Edinburgh Review. But I think he must see that he identifies me with

the accusation, if it be one, of the Reviewer,
when he uses such a turn of expression as
"the Reviewer should have remembered that
to praise an accuser is to share the responsibility of the accusation."

I most emphatically deny that I have made
anything approaching to "a charge of Atheism"
against Mr. Mansel. I have expressly complimented him, at the conclusion of my Postscript,
on the power of statement which he exhibits in
vindicating the representation of God given in
the Bible from a certain class of objections:
and I have as expressly admitted the happy
inconsistency which appears between the doctrines advocated by him as a philosopher, and
his own religious sentiments as displayed in
the more rhetorical passages of his work. All
that I have said has reference not to his personal
convictions, much less to his personal character,
but solely to the doctrines put forth in his book.
I say of those doctrines, in the words of Clarke,
that "if we argue upon them consistently, we
must finally recur to absolute Atheism." If I
may not be allowed to say this, as a most
eminent and excellent man said it before me,
I do not see how it is possible to take up any
position in the matter. Suppose a theory to
be put forward tending, as a matter of fact, to

atheistical consequences, are we to be forbidden to point out these consequences, on
pain of being told that we have committed a
breach of good manners by calling the author
of the theory an atheist? If so, there are
some parts of Mr. Mansel's own book in which
he is guilty of breaches of good manners.

Mr. Mansel states that his delay in replying
to me was caused by his not having read my
remarks, though he was "early made aware"
that they had been published. How was it
that those who made him aware of the publication failed to inform him that I had made
"imputations under which no man would
"remain longer than he could help?"

To prove that I am not guilty of calumny
or the victim of an hallucination in saying
that the tendency of Mr. Mansel's doctrines is
atheistical, I appeal to Mr. Herbert Spencer's
work on "First Principles." Mr. Mansel will
there find his own doctrines adopted in his own
words as the foundation stone of a great system
of philosophy, which he and I should agree in
calling atheistical, by a very acute and honest
writer. Mr. Spencer even thinks that Mr.
Mansel's scepticism is too exterminating; and
that certain qualifications must be introduced
in deference to the religious instincts of man-

kind. The passage of Mr. Spencer's work to which I refer is :—

"There still remains the final question—What must we say concerning that which transcends knowledge? Are we to rest wholly in the consciousness of phenomena? — is the result of inquiry to exclude utterly from our minds everything but the relative? or must we also believe in something beyond the relative?

"The answer of pure logic is held to be, that by the limits of our intelligence we are rigorously confined within the relative; and that anything transcending the relative can be thought of only as a pure negation, or a non-existence. 'The *absolute* is conceived merely by a negation of conceivability,' writes Sir William Hamilton. 'The *Absolute* and the *Infinite*,' says Mr. Mansel, 'are thus, like the *Inconceivable* and the *Imperceptible*, names indicating, not an object of thought or of consciousness at all, but the mere absence of the conditions under which consciousness is possible.' From each of which extracts may be deduced the conclusion, that since reason cannot warrant us in affirming the positive existence of what is cognizable only as a negation, we cannot rationally affirm the positive existence of anything beyond phenomena.

"Unavoidable as this conclusion seems, it involves, I think, an error. If the premiss be granted, the inference must doubtless be admitted; but the premiss, in the form presented by Sir William Hamilton and Mr. Mansel, is not strictly true. Though, in the foregoing pages, the arguments used by these writers to shew that the Absolute is unknowable, have been approvingly quoted; and though these arguments have been enforced by others equally thoroughgoing ; yet there remains to be stated a qualification, which saves us from that scepticism otherwise necessitated." (*First Principles*, p. 87.)

I appeal also to an article in the *Revue des Deux Mondes* on "Natural Theology in England," the author of which is M. Charles de Remusat. In this article, Mr. Mansel is highly complimented on the ability displayed in his book, but is significantly warned that the shafts

of scepticism are apt to recoil upon him who
shoots them, and is told that, "though he will
probably not be attacked as Dr. Hampden was,
his doctrine, in its full application, will probably inflict a severer blow than Dr. Hampden
inflicted on scholastic formularies and creeds,"
and that "he has, in fact, devoted his tempo-
rary occupancy of a theological chair to the
task of proving that there is no such thing as
theology." [1]

If I cannot help thinking that Mr. Mansel
displayed occasional misgivings as to the effect
of particular arguments to which he had committed himself, I do not for a moment doubt
that he was entirely free from any misgiving
as to the general effect of his book. Unques-
tionably he thought he was doing good service
to the Church by destroying the foundations of
Rational Religion. At the same time he will
not think it strange if I hold and endeavour
to prove that he has unconsciously done good
service to Rational Religion by showing that

---

[1] "C'est par les *Bampton Lectures* que le révérend Henri
Mansel introduit une doctrine qui ne lui vaudra pas les mêmes
attaques qu'au docteur Hampden, mais qui, suivie dans toutes
ses applications, pourrait bien atteindre plus gravement les formu-
laires et les confessions de foi libellées en termes d'école, car au
fond M. Mansel a consacré son court passage dans une chaire de
théologie à démontrer qu'il n'y a pas de théologie."—*Revue des
Deux Mondes*, vol. 25, p. 564.

an irrational theory of religion logically tends to atheism; and that man must use the reason which God has given him in order to attain the knowledge of God.

Few controversialists are more unsparing, as few are more powerful, in exposing the errors of their antagonists than Mr. Mansel; and he must not suppose that there is one law for those who err in defence of orthodoxy, and another for those who err in the pursuit of truth.

OXFORD, OCTOBER, 1861.

POSTSCRIPT TO LECTURE ON THE
STUDY OF HISTORY. No. II.

THE doctrine of Clarke as to the identity of human and divine justice, to which I have subscribed [1] and without which it seems to me that history and the whole moral world would be reduced to chaos, is controverted, in the supposed interest of revealed religion, by the learned and distinguished author of the Bampton Lectures for 1858, who (p. 206, 3rd ed.) comes to the conclusion that "human morality, even in its highest elevation, is not identical with, nor adequate to measure, the Absolute Morality of God." If this be so, I venture to submit, with Clarke, that the "morality of God" is an utterly unmeaning phrase. or that, if it means anything, it means the *immorality* of God ; human morality and human immorality being the only two ideas which our minds can possibly form upon the subject, or which our language can possibly express.

[1] See Lectures " On the Study of History," p. 60, and the Preface to the present publication.

If there are two moralities, a Divine and a Human, which may indefinitely conflict with each other (and as we "are unable to fix in any human conception" what the divine morality is, we cannot fix any definite limit to their conflict,) there is, in effect, no morality at all.

Elsewhere (p. 244,) the Lecturer, in spite of his decision that the moralities of God and man are not identical, shows a desire to reconcile divine with human morality in regard to certain actions attributed to God, of which the morality is disputed. This he does by introducing a doctrine of moral miracles, which isolates the actions in question from the divine nature and character, and thus saves the divine morality in human eyes. It would have been more consistent to say that the actions, being instances of divine, not of human morality, were not to be reconciled with our moral perceptions. A miracle in the ordinary sense is a breach of the natural law : a moral miracle, by analogy, must be a breach of the moral law. Why should not a criminal at the bar, instead of making a bad defence, say that he has performed a moral miracle ?

"That there is an Absolute Morality, based upon, or rather identical with, the Eternal Nature of God," says the Lecturer, in a passage immediately preceding that which I first quoted, " is indeed a conviction forced upon us by the same evidence as that on which we believe that God exists at all. But *what* that Absolute Morality is we are as unable to fix in any human conception as we are to define the other attributes of the same Divine Nature." To believe in the existence of that which we " are unable to fix in any human conception," and to believe in its relation to and identity with another thing (which, according to the Lecturer, is equally beyond our conception), will, I believe, be found, on the most conscientious experiment, a feat impossible to the human mind. The " conviction" may be " forced" upon the Lecturer, if he wishes to avoid the tremendous consequences of his theory, but he cannot, without giving us new understandings, " force" it upon us.

By thus denying the identity of Human and Divine morality, we cut away, as Clarke truly observes, all arguments for the immortality of the soul which are founded on divine justice. If we know nothing of the absolute justice of God, what presumption is there that it will lead Him to redress the sufferings of the good in a future state of existence ?

It fares with truth as with morality. " The highest principles of thought and action, to which we can attain, are *regulative*, not *speculative* ; they do not serve to satisfy the reason, but to

guide the conduct ; they do not tell us what
things are in themselves, but how we must conduct ourselves in relation to them."—(p. 141.)
" It is thus strictly in analogy with the method of
God's Providence in the constitution of man's
mental faculties, if we believe that in religion also
He has given us truths which are designed to be
regulative rather than speculative ; intended not to
satisfy our reason, but to guide our practice ; not
to tell us what God is in His absolute nature, but
how He wills that we should think of Him in
our present finite state."—(p. 143.) If there is
no truth attainable by man but " regulative
truth," there is no truth attainable by man at all.
" Regulative truth" is a nonentity. A *rule* may
be such as it is necessary to obey, but it cannot, in
the proper sense, be *true*. Is not the substitution
of the uncommon and incorrect phrase " regulative
truth" for the common word " rule," prompted by
an instinctive reluctance to exhibit the terrible
image of an Almighty Master in place of a moral
God ?

It may be true that " action and not knowledge
is man's destiny and duty in this life."—(p. 149.)
But that to which the Lecturer reduces the state of
man is action *without* knowledge ; the state of
mere physical agents.

That " there is a higher and unchangeable

principle embodied in these forms" (p. 209) is a welcome doctrine ; but to say that we " have abundant reason to believe it" is to assume that we not only can attain, but transcend, the limits of the highest " speculative" truth.   It is to assume that we can pronounce not only on the existence but on the " embodiment" in certain forms of that which " we are unable to fix in any human conception."

Morality and truth are gone, and God hardly remains. If God is " inconceivable" (p. 171) I fail to apprehend how we can believe in Him : my mind, though conjured in the name of " duty," is unable to present to itself the existence of anything of which I have no conception. Still more obvious does it seem to me that I cannot, with the nature that is given me, revere and love a Being who reveals Himself to me, not as He is, but under " regulative representations." — (p. 150.)   The Lecturer, indeed, (p. 145,) lays it down as matter of " faith" that " the conceptions which we are compelled to adopt as the guides of our thoughts and actions now, may indeed, in the sight of a higher Intelligence, be but partial truth, but cannot be total falsehood."   God's own representation of Himself to man cannot be *totally false* ! Why not *totally* false as well as *partly* false ?   Who has assured the Lecturer that the " conceptions" which we are " compelled to adopt" bear to the reality any relation expressible by the human terms 'truth' and 'falsehood'? But supposing it to be ascertained that they are only in part false; how are we to know which part is the truth, which the falsehood? To what are our hearts to turn as the real object of our religious affection? From what are they to turn away (they cannot choose but turn away) as the "falsehood" and the mask?

Is the Church of England prepared to say of Christ that He was to the Apostles a 'regulative representation,' 'not *totally* false,' of the Divine Nature?

In asserting that conceptions which God compels man to adopt cannot be total falsehood, the Lecturer, it seems to me, is doing that which he warns us against presuming to do: he is constructing "a Philosophy of the Absolute.' He is, in like manner, constructing a philosophy of the Absolute when he undertakes to say (p. 242) that "it is one thing to condemn a religion on account of the habitual observance of licentious or inhuman rites of worship, and another to pronounce judgment on isolated facts, historically recorded as having been done by divine command, but not perpetuated in precepts for the imitation of posterity." How, but by transcending what he lays down as the limits of human thought, can he be assured that the difference between the Divine and the Diabolical nature is this, that whereas the Diabolical nature is habitually criminal, the Divine nature commits only isolated crimes ?

If he says that it is the "regulative" ill effect of habitually inhuman and licentious religions that proves them not to be divine, where but in a Philosophy of the Absolute does he find the sanction of that particular criterion ? From what other source can he have learnt that "facts" "done by divine command," though not expressly "perpetuated in precepts," are not intended "for the imitation of posterity ?" He tells us (p. 211) that "there are limits within which alone " the rule of the suspension of human duties by God " can be *safely* applied." Is "safely" to be taken as having reference to our personal convenience, or to what he is taught by the philosophy of the Absolute respecting the nature of things ?

In another place (p. 240) the Lecturer says, " We are indeed bound to believe that a revelation given by God can never contain anything that is really unwise or unrighteous." Here, again, he seems to be constructing a philosophy of the Absolute. " Real wisdom " and " real righteousness " must be used in a sense intelligible to us, or we could not possibly be " bound " to have any belief about them ; but without a philosophy of the Absolute how can we tell that everything

in a revelation given by God must be really wise
and righteous in a sense intelligible to us ? The
"duty" implied in the word "bound" can have
its sanction only in that philosophy which the
Lecturer has declared to be impossible.

There is one passage of the lectures in which,
if I do not misapprehend its import, a belief[1] in
God is actually proved to be impossible to the
human mind. "Sensation without thought would
at most amount to no more than an indefinite sense
of uneasiness or momentary irritation, without any
power of discerning in what manner we are affected,
or of distinguishing our successive affections from
each other. To distinguish, for example, in the
visible world, any one object from any other, to
know the house as a house, or the tree as a tree, we
must be able to refer them to distinct notions ; and
such reference is an act of thought. The same
condition holds good of the religious consciousness
also. In whatever mental affection we become

---

[1] Mr. Mansel has charged me with having here substituted *belief*
for *conception* for the purpose of "adding point to denunciation." I
am stating my own impression as to the effect of Mr. Mansel's
reasoning, and I am entitled to state it in my own words. Both here
and elsewhere, Mr. Mansel will observe, I take him to have proved
a good deal more than he intended. *His* reasoning is not only "expressed as nearly as possible in his own language" which he says
"justice requires," but given in his own words. I should have found,
however, no warrant in the passage for the use of *conception* as ex-
pressive of Mr. Mansel's opinion. The material words are *consciousness* and *existence*.

conscious of our relation to a Supreme Being, we can discern that consciousness, as such, only by reflecting upon it as conceived under its proper notion. Without this, we could not know our religious consciousness to be what it is; and, as the knowledge of a fact of consciousness is identical with its existence, without this, the religious consciousness, as such, could not exist."—(p. 197.) Is there any "proper notion" analogous to the "notion" of a "house" under which our relation to a Supreme Being can be conceived? And if there is none, does it not follow from the Lecturer's reasoning that this "fact of religious consciousness" cannot be known, and therefore that it cannot exist? Is not the argument in effect this—'We can have no distinct knowledge of anything, unless we can refer it to a class of objects, and thus distinguish it in our minds from objects of a different class, and that of which we have no distinct knowledge has to our minds no existence. Now there is no class of objects to which we can properly refer God; therefore we can have no distinct knowledge of God; therefore to our minds God has no existence.' In his apologetic Preface (p. xix.) the Lecturer says, "A negative idea by no means implies a negation of all mental activity. It implies an attempt to think, and a failure in accomplishing the attempt." But I presume it also implies a failure to love, revere, and commune with that which is a mere negative idea. And, what the Lecturer does not seem to observe, it implies a failure to recognise or receive any sort of revelation. Revelation is the voice of God. How can we know the voice, if the Speaker is unknown ?

Again, when we are told (p. 144) in regard to our capability of knowing God, that, "we behold effects only, and not causes," the natural import of this expression surely is, that we are cognizant of creation only, not of a Creator. I do not wonder that materialists should have received these lectures with approbation, as well as Bishops. It is to blank materialism and empiricism that such reasonings inevitably lead.

Morality, truth, God, are swept away. Nothing is left but the bare, hard text of Scripture, as a brazen regulator thrust into the world by an almighty Power, to compel us to move in a certain way, without reference to the moral reason which God has given us, however rash some divines may think it in Him to have done so. And this "relative truth" has been inserted into the world piece by piece, at long intervals of time. A portion of truth is truth ; but a fragment of a rule is no rule at all.

· Is such a revelation as this a revelation indeed, or an obscuration of God ?

Scripture is not to commend itself by the divine character of its contents, for this would be making men able to discern and appreciate what is divine. " The legitimate object of a rational criticism of revealed religion is not to be found in the *contents* of that religion, but in its *evidences*."—(p. 234.) And the only evidences left to us, it would seem, are the miracles, considered as exhibitions of power. To consider them as exhibitions of divine love, and put them forward as evidences in that respect, would be to construct a philosophy of the Absolute ; for it would be to assume that love, human love, is divine, and its exhibitions a note of divinity. All the internal evidences fall under the same fatal objection ; being all moral, they all involve the assumption that human morality is identical with the morality of God. The miracles, as evidences of power, alone remain ; and the Scripture itself says that miracles of power may be diabolical as well as divine.

If the words of Scripture are "regulative representations" of the divine nature, and if the moral notions signified by them are not our moral notions, they will become rather sacred amulets than words. Their sanctity and efficacy will depend on their exact identity. Can we be certain that they will bear translation into another human language ? What becomes of the Gospel of St.

Matthew, and the Epistle to the Hebrews, which have probably not been transmitted to us in the original tongue ? Can we venture to interpret the "regulative representation" of the inconceivable ? or must we simply keep it with reverence as an *ancile* which has fallen from the skies? Deductions from Scripture seem to be quite out of the question. At one point (p. 2.) the Lecturer is seized with a just misgiving that his scythe has swept away the Athanasian Creed. He therefore throws in a saving clause for "the mere enunciation of religious truths, as resting upon authority, and not upon reasoning." But what is this " authority," and how is it established ? Is it in possession of a philosophy of the Absolute, that it should be able to say which among the " regulative representations " of Scripture are a proper subject for the human process of deduction ? Further on (p. 5) the Lecturer stigmatizes as dogmatists[1] those "who seek to build up a complete scheme of theological doctrine out of the unsystematic materials furnished by Scripture, partly by the more complete development of certain leading

---

[1] Mr. Mansel tells me angrily that "Dogmatism and Rationalism were not introduced into his lectures for the purpose of being stigmatized." The opening words of his book are, "Dogmatism and Rationalism are the two extremes between which religious philosophy perpetually oscillates. Each represents a system, from which, when nakedly and openly announced, the well-regulated mind almost instinctively shrinks back ; yet which, in some more or less specious disguise, will be found to underlie the antagonist positions of many a theological

ideas; partly by extending the apparent import of the Revelation to ground which it does not avowedly occupy, and attempting by inference and analogy to solve problems which the sacred volume may indeed suggest, but which it does not directly answer; partly by endeavouring to give additional support to the scriptural statements themselves, treating them as truths, not above, but within the grasp of reason, and capable of demonstration from rational premises." Repudiate " the development of leading ideas," " the extension of the apparent import of revelation," " the solution by inference or ana- logy of problems suggested but not answered by the sacred volume," and what justification is left for the framers of the Athanasian Creed, not to say of the Nicene ? I should have thought that the passage was directly intended to cut away every possible ground from under their feet. When we take up " weapons " in defence of a good cause, we must take care that they have not a double edge.

You go to a heathen whom you wish to convert, and say, ' You must not judge of my religion by its contents, for they are beyond your judgment, but

controversy." And in the very passage from which I am quoting, and to which my remarks refer, he lays it down as his basis that " in rela- tion to the actual condition of religious truth, as communicated by Holy Scriptures, Dogmatism and Rationalism may be considered as severally representing *the one the spirit which adds to the Word of God and the other that which diminishes from it."* Surely here, at all events, Dogmatism is " stigmatized."

E

14

by its evidences, which are the miracles,' May not
he answer, 'My religion is said to be attested by
miracles as well as yours, and the questions of historical criticism, on the one side and on the other, are
such as I have neither time, learning, nor capacity
to solve. Besides, according to your own Scriptures, Egyptian sorcerers and false prophets can
perform miracles, so that I do not see how miracles
by themselves can establish the truth of a religion.'
Or rather, supposing him to have any notion of
religion, would he not say, 'If your religion is to be
judged, not by its contents, but by its evidences, it
must be the lowest and vilest religion in the world.'

Spinoza, in his *Tractatus Theologico-Politicus*
(c. 15), after setting forth the discrepancy between
Scripture and reason, proceeds to consider their
relative claims. One party, he says, bend Scripture
to reason; another party bend reason to Scripture.[1]
He rejects both these courses, and concludes, "quod
nec theologia rationi, nec ratio theologiæ ancillari
teneatur, sed unaquæque suum regnum obtineat;
nempe uti diximus, ratio regnum veritatis et sa-

[1] I have altered this sentence so as to waive all questions touching Spinoza's peculiar use of the terms "Sceptics" and "Dogmatists." They are immaterial to the quotations which it is my only
object to introduce. No doubt, however, Mr. Mansel is right on
this point. In his anxiety to frame an indictment against his own
moral character, he has included "Mephistophelic language of the
Arch-Pantheist" among the things which I have said of *his* doctrines
— (Letter, p. 46.)

pientiæ, theologia autem pietatis et obedientiæ."
He has before (c. 13) demonstrated to his own
satisfaction, "Scripturam non nisi simplicissima docere, nec aliud præter obedientiam intendere; nec
de divina natura aliud docere, quam quod homines
certa vivendi ratione imitari possunt." The Mephistophelic language of the Arch-pantheist seems in a
fair way to become the orthodox theory of revelation.

Any attempt to determine the relative spiritual
value of the different parts of the regulative truth
contained in the Scriptures, becomes as vain and
rash as interpretation and deduction. "Not only
"if you reject one jot or one tittle of the whole doctrine of Christ" must you pronounce the whole an
imposture, (p. 249) but if you doubt the literal
accuracy or the perfect authenticity of one jot or
one tittle of any part of the Bible, the authority of
the whole is gone "We may not divide God's
Revelation."[1] A trifling discrepancy, a passage

---

[1] In this application of Mr. Mansel's language, again, I am said to
have been guilty of "extensive misrepresentation." The passage of his
lecture to which I alluded ran—"Either He was what he proclaimed
Himself to be—the incarnate Son of God, the Divine Saviour of a fallen
world—and, if so, we may not divide God's Revelation, and dare to
put asunder what He has joined together, or" &c. He now puts "*if so*"
in italics, but surely he does not mean that the *if* expresses doubt.
So far from attempting to limit the principle implied in the words,
"we may not divide God's Revelation," he, in his letter to me, expressly avows that it "is applicable to Scripture as a whole." What
wrong then have I done him in so applying it? "You go on,"
he says, "to tell me that the Church of Rome includes the Apocrypha
in the Canon." And he asks me "whether this is criticism or carica-

of questionable genuineness, may deprive Man of Revelation and of God.

But the most formidable difficulty still remains. If the exact canon of Scripture is everything, what is the exact canon of Scripture, and who is its appointed guardian? Philosophy, we are told," speaks with stammering lips and a double tongue." The voice of the Churches is not perfectly clear or one. The Church of Rome includes the Apocrypha in the necessary sum of "regulative truth." The Church of England pronounces for their exclusion. There are no miracles to decide the question; and the Lecturer is a man of too much sense to suppose that it can be decided for each man by the accident of his birth. As to the Anglican Canon, the Article, we know, states that there never was any doubt in the church about the authority of any of the books contained in it. But the histories which contradict the Article as to the matter of fact require elaborate confutation. If we can know God, and know His voice, these difficulties are as nothing; if we cannot know God, they are death.

Finally, Scripture itself is directly at issue with the philosophy, or negation of philosophy, on which,

ture." I "go on" in a separate paragraph to put, as my own, a dilemma arising out of the differences between different Churches respecting the Canon, which, I think, he will not easily evade. This, in my opinion, is "criticism," and it is not my fault if the theory which I am criticizing, when pushed to its legitimate consequences, looks very like a 'caricature.'

according to the Lecturer, its exclusive authority is founded. It sets out with the declaration, the solemn and repeated declaration, that man was created in the image of his Maker; whereas the negative philosophy proves that the morality of man is not identical with the absolute morality of God, and consequently that the moral nature of God cannot be imaged in that of man. The Author of Christianity bids us pray God to forgive us our trespasses as we forgive them that trespass against us; a direct appeal to an analogy between the human and divine nature. On the other hand, the Bampton Lecturer says (p. 214) that " it is obvious on a moment's reflection, that the duty of man to forgive the trespasses of his neighbour rests precisely upon those features of human nature which cannot by any analogy be regarded as representing an image of God." I have read what the Lecturer has said in his answer to Mr. Maurice, but there is no escaping the contradiction. The clause in the Lord's Prayer is not an appeal to human sinfulness, but to Divine sympathy, and to a similarity, in the act of free forgiveness, between the human nature and the Divine. The Lecturer's inflexible logic has led him into a dilemma not unlike those into which the great Jesuit doctors were led (most innocently as I believe) through their unwary reasonings from premises originally commended rather by their adaptation to the weakness of human nature than by their abstract truth.

Let it be at once said, however, that throughout these Lectures, with the dark growth of the negative philosophy, there twines, in happy contradiction, a more wholesome plant, attesting the real geniality of the soil beneath. In the more rhetorical passages (as at p. 190) the Christian preacher gives the cold doctrines of the negative philosopher to the winds, and admits implicitly that there are firm, independent grounds for natural religion. Again, (at p. 248,) he places among the evidences of Christianity the character of its Founder; whose portrait he there, embracing the better philosophy, acknowledges that we can pronounce to be Divine.

It is therefore the less necessary to follow him into the metaphysical labyrinth which he has constructed for himself and his hearers. By turning a notion really negative, such as "infinity," into a positive notion, and bringing it into antagonism with its supposed opposite, you may make mental puzzles enough for a long summer's day. The soundest as well as the simplest way of approaching the question is to begin by enquiring, not whether there can be a Philosophy of the Absolute or of the Infinite, but whether the pure in heart see God.

I will add two remarks, which, perhaps, occur to me especially as a student of history.

The first remark is this. The blow which in these Lectures kills natural religion is dealt through the side of German philosophy. I am quite prepared to believe that German philosophy is scholasticism, not science; that it reasons from arbitrary notions; and that it has borne, and will bear, no fruit. It is, perhaps, neither the only nor the last philosophy of which this might be plausibly affirmed. If it founds religion on pure metaphysics and logic, it falls into an absurdity equalled only by that of attempting to prove the impossibility of religion on purely metaphysical or logical grounds. But history owes it thanks for a great and noble effort to give Europe a moral faith at a time when all faith had been swept away by the corruption of the clergy and the destructive criticism of Voltaire. Fichte may have run into extravagances; but think that he devoted his intellect to the support of a high, disinterested morality in the age of Talleyrand and Bishop Prettyman, and you will be inclined, if you can be touched by the weakness of humanity, to strew flowers upon his grave.

The second remark is this. Before you decide, on metaphysical grounds, to what degree of religious knowledge man can attain, it may be useful to enquire, historically, what degree he has actually attained. It may be well to consider the natural religion of Plato, and still more that of Marcus Aurelius and Epictetus, before you pronounce that no natural religion is possible, beyond a blind craving for support and expiation. History, without moral philosophy, is a mere string of facts; and moral philosophy, without history, is apt to become a dream.

Nor, while I adhere to the doctrine opposed to that of the Lecturer, in regard to his main position, will I conclude these brief observations on his theory without paying the humble tribute of my sincere admiration to the power of statement displayed in some parts of his book. I may allude especially to a passage in his first lecture, where, in vindicating the representation of God given in the Bible, he demolishes the figment, much in vogue among exclusively scientific minds, of an insensible, inflexible, immovable, in a word, of a scientific, as opposed to a moral, God. It is one thing to use controversial weapons borrowed from negative philosophy; it is another thing to be yourself a negative philosopher.

DEFENCE

Mr. Mansel must by this time have begun to be aware that the doctrines propounded in his Lectures lead to consequences of a startling kind. 'He tells me indeed that, " to attack a doctrine on account of its consequences is a method which is very easy and applicable to both sides of most controversies." But I must beg his pardon. No doctrine can be fairly reduced to absurdity which is not intrinsically absurd. No doctrine can be fairly reduced to atheism which is not intrinsically atheistic. It is not in every polemical treatise that we can really see the Nemesis of Orthodoxy which has borrowed weapons from Rationalism to destroy Rational Religion.

Instead of clearing up the difficulties of his Lectures and relieving our misgivings by explanation, Mr. Mansel has chosen, in his Letter to me, to defend his theory by compurgation. His great learning has filled the pages of a long pamphlet with quotations from writers who, he

F

alleges, held the opinions or something like the opinions which are now called in question. The issue which he wishes to tender to us is not whether his views are sound and compatible with the existence of religion, but whether they have or have not been entertained by certain other persons.

On my own behalf, and on behalf of all who are interested in the discussion, I must decline this issue as irrelevant and unprofitable.

I take my stand on the principle enunciated by Mr. Mansel himself, which I have adopted as my motto,—'It is of little importance by what authority an opinion is sanctioned, if it will not itself stand the test of sound criticism.' The use of learning is to enable its possessor to form right opinions. When he has formed and published them, he must be prepared to answer for them as his own, and to defend them with his own arguments, not with other men's names.

The attempt to decide questions in philosophy by polling authorities on either side would be interminable and hopeless. We should have to begin by fixing a standard of authority : and to come to an agreement on that standard would always be at least as difficult as to come to an agreement on the original question. In the present instance, for example, there would be a difference of opinion between my opponent and me at the outset. I recognise only two sources of authority, the moral and the intellectual : he recognises others.

It is evident that he attributes a special authority of a very high and even overwhelming kind to Episcopal rank. He cites the testimony even of Dr. Hampden with complacency, as that of a "prelate ;" holding, apparently, that accession to a mitre purges away heresy, as accession to the Crown was held in the case of Henry VII. to purge away attainder. He extends the authority of Bishops from ecclesiastical to philosophical questions. He extends it even beyond their lives. He feels it necessary formally to apologize for quoting a passage which may be thought to have reflected upon a prelate even after the lapse of more than a hundred years.[1] I trust I am not wanting in respect for those who, by their eminent virtues, the cautious character of their theological convictions, and the coincidence of their political opinions with those of the First Minister, backed in many instances by assiduous and judicious solicitation, have been raised to the highest preferment in the Established Church. But to me an Episcopal philosopher is a philosopher and nothing more : to me, a dead bishop is a dead man.

Mr. Mansel also attributes special authority to

[1] See " A Letter, &c." p. 8. I was half inclined to take the passage as ironical, but I believe it is serious.

those who lived "in the days of the giants of theology." I hold with Bacon *antiquitas sæculi juventus mundi*, and venerate the great men of former times as intellectual ancestors and benefactors, not as gods. The bones of the "giants" of former days have been found, and they measure no more than ours.

When the general standard of authority has been fixed, there comes the question whether the particular authority alleged in each case is actually in point. To pronounce in the affirmative, we must be assured that the writer had before him the exact question at present in issue, which, from the restless flow of thought, is seldom the case; and we must be assured of the precise meaning of his words, which, if disputed, can be settled only by a general induction from his works. We ought also to know the historical circumstances under which he wrote, that we may be able to estimate the effects of those circumstances on his mind and to make allowance for the bias which they may have given to his thoughts. Butler, for instance, would smile or weep to see the little parasitic imitators of his philosophy arguing against the sincere and pure-minded inquirers of the present day in the style in which he argued against the libertine free-thinkers of his own time.

Some of Mr. Mansel's compurgators are brought

into court for him with reluctance, and give very
faltering evidence when they are there.

No distinction is made in his citations between
philosophical and rhetorical passages. To prove
the philosophical paradox that thought and belief
are not co-extensive, and that we may be bound to
believe in that which we cannot fix in any human
conception, he cites the rhetorical passage of Hooker,
" Dangerous.it were for the feeble brain of man to
wade far into the doings of the Most High ; whom
although to know be life, and joy to make mention of
His name; yet our soundest knowledge is to know
that we know Him not as indeed He is, neither can
know Him, and our safest eloquence concerning Him
is our silence, when we confess without confession that
His glory is inexplicable, His greatness above our
capacity and reach." To prove the same point, he
cites another passage from the ' Confessions ' of St.
Augustine, the very form of which glaringly betrays
its rhetorical character—" Nam sicut omnino tu es,
tu scis solus, qui es incommutabiliter, et scis incom-
mutalibiter, et vis incommutabiliter." It did not
occur to him in citing the passage from Hooker,
that he might himself be " wading " as " far "
into " the doings of the Most High " in maintaining that the Divine morality was different from
the human as those do who maintain that man was
created in the image of God. Not every doctrine

is humility in the preacher which is humiliating to man.

In tendering rhetoric as philosophy, Mr. Mansel does not show much respect for the penetration of his readers. I think he scarcely shows more in tendering them, as evidence of the difference between Divine and human morality, a long extract from a loosely worded discourse of Bishop Copleston. That prelate, in one sentence, forbids us " to indulge the notion that the admirable and estimable qualities of men are really *like* to the corresponding qualities in God." In the next sentence he subscribes to the opinion that " any qualities that are estimable and praiseworthy in men are *dim shadows* and *faint communications* of those attributes which exist in God in complete and adorable perfection." As though it were possible for one thing to be a *communication* of another without being *really like* it ; and as though one thing could be at once the *shadow* of another and its *communication*. Bishop Copleston was, it seems, of opinion, upon 'attentive consideration' of the question, that the objection of his opponents to his view of the Divine Nature arose 'not so much from a jealousy for the honor of God, to which it pretended, as from a jealousy for the honor of man ?' There is yet a third interest, for the honor of which a due amount of jealousy is often felt, but which the Bishop had not the advantage of regarding from an independent point of view.

Archbishop Whately is also cited to testify that human morality is not identical with the Divine. But I think this citation only proves the inconvenience of making people parties to a controversy which has not been brought fully before them. The material part of the quotation is this :

" For, 1st, when two persons (or other objects) are said to have the *same* quality, accident, &c. what we predicate of them is evidently a certain *resemblance*, and nothing else. ...... 2dly, such qualities as are entirely *relative*,—which consists in the relation borne by the subject to certain other things,—in this it is manifest that the only *resemblance* that *can* exist is *resemblance of relations*, i. e. ANALOGY. Courage, *e. g.* consists in the relation in which one stands towards dangers..... When it is said, therefore, of two courageous men, that they have both the *same* quality, the only meaning this expression *can* have is, that they are, so far, completely *analogous* in their characters ; having similar ratios to certain similar objects .... Thus it appears that what Dr. King has been so vehemently censured for denying concerning the Deity, is literally true even with respect to men themselves ; *viz.* that it is only by Analogy that two persons can be said to possess the same virtue, or other such quality. 3dly, But what he means is, plainly, that this analogy is far less *exact and complete* in the case of a comparison between the Deity and his creatures, than between one man and another : which surely no one would venture to deny."

What the Archbishop here in effect denies is not the identity of the Divine and human attributes as qualities, which is the question now in issue, but their numerical identity. 'Two men,' he says, cannot have the same courage; each must have a courage of his own : and in the same way the Deity and a man both cannot have the same virtue. He implicitly admits that a man may have the same quality with the Deity in the same sense in which he can have the same virtue with another man. It is for the Archbishop to make it clear that in saying this he has said anything very instructive: but this it is, and not anything more apposite to Mr. Mansel's purpose, that he has said.

By culling the bad passages from good authors we might make up a set of opinions compared with which all the absurdities in any one bad author would be a rational creed. To prove that conception and belief are not co-extensive, Mr. Mansel quotes from Barrow the words, " If all concerning God be thus incomprehensible, why should any thing seem incredible ? Why, out of so many inconceivable mysteries, do we choose some, reprobate others?" Mr. Mansel himself " is not prepared to receive this strange language "unconditionally," but he is prepared to take advantage of any shelter it may afford him. He "believes it to be at least far nearer to the truth than the opposite assertion." But surely between two contradictory propositions in the strict science of psychology there can be no room for comparative nearness to the truth.

In a quotation from Beveridge, which fills two thirds of a page relating to the same point, the material word is a mere equivoque. " I cannot *conceive* it, though I verily *believe* it, how He is of

Himself infinitely holy, just, powerful. Yet I can easily *conceive* how He is without body, parts, and passions," &c. Here, *conceive* evidently has not the logical sense corresponding to the logical term *conception*. It is used, somewhat improperly, for *understand*. Had the Bampton Lectures for 1858 been laid before Beveridge, I should have been glad to hear his opinion as to their agreement with his view of religion.

To come to the point, then. Mr. Mansel, in his lectures, has arrived at the conclusion that " human morality, even in its highest elevation, is not identical with, nor adequate to measure, the Absolute Morality of God." I said, and I adhere to the opinion, that, if this be so, the " Morality of God " is an unmeaning phrase, or, if it means anything, means the *immorality* of God; human morality and human immorality being the only two ideas which our minds can possibly form upon the subject, or which our language can possibly express. That actions or sentiments which differ from our morality in the same moral matter are to us immoral, and that if we speak sincerely, we must call them so, is a position which, I apprehend, cannot easily be assailed. Nor has Mr. Mansel attempted to give us any satisfaction on this point, or to show us that his doctrine does not threaten confusion to the moral world.

G

He desires I will tell him, "if the morality of
God is identical with human morality, wherein that
identity consists;" and "what I mean when I
assert that the two moralities are identical with
each other." Surely this is a little unreasonable
on his part. Surely it is for him to help our minds
to the apprehension of two moralities (the phrase is
his own) different from each other, and of acts
which may be at once immoral according to the
morality of man, and moral according to the
morality of God. I can only say that I labour,
and that I believe the mass of mankind labour,
under an absolute inability to represent to themselves in any way whatever any morality but one.
The theory of a single morality is at least the ordinary theory. It is in possession, and may challenge
opponents to displace it. Every unsophisticated
mind turns to God in the belief that the Divine
morality is the source and perfection, and can
never be the contradiction, of its own. I might
fill not only a book, but a library, with quotations
from Anglican Divines setting forth the Divine
attributes, and vindicating them to man on the
implicit assumption that they are the same in
kind as those which constitute the better part of
human nature, and that the hearts of the hearers
or readers will accordingly respond to the appeal.
The essence of morality is the love of our neigh-

bour, as the essence of religion is the love of God. If Mr. Mansel desires me to shew him how Divine and human love can be the same, I can only refer him, as a Christian and a philosopher, to the concluding chapters of the Gospel of St. John. There he will find also framed for him what he challenges me to prove "a clear conception of the essence of morality apart from all relation to the constitution of the human mind on the circumstances of human life," if by that constitution and those circumstances he means anything which will pass away with the transitory order of this world. It is dangerous, when you are constructing a philosophical theory of Christianity, to be too "fresh from the study" of those divines of the eighteenth century, whose religious philosophy sometimes is little better than heathenism without freedom of thought, and Christianity without Christ.

Mr. Mansel suggests that I may get out of the dilemma into which he has put me, by saying "that there is a common principle of morality running through" both the moralities, the human and the Divine. This he says he believes also; but he adds the perplexing words that "the common principle is not human morality; it is morality with the human element removed." I have stated my own position, which is, that

there is no morality imaginable by the human
mind or which can be the subject of human
belief, but one. But had I admitted that there
were " two moralities," that one of them was
" Absolute," and that the " Absolute" indicated
" not an object of thought or consciousness at
all, but the mere absence of the conditions
under which consciousness was possible," I
should think it quite beyond my power to pronounce that there was a common principle running through the morality which was known to
us, and that of which we could not even be
conscious. I do not see how I could attempt
to maintain this without constructing a " Philosophy of the Absolute " of the most presumptuous
kind.

A " principle," which is " morality with the human element removed," and which " runs through"
human morality, and another morality which, by
the hypothesis, is not a possible object of thought
or consciousness —this, I confess, seems to me
darkness as profound as German Philosophy in
its most mystic hour has ever presented to the
bewildered mind of man.

What the principle common to human and Divine
morality is ; what is its extent ; and how far we
are empowered to reason on it ;—are questions on
the determination of which the very life of the

moral world must turn. The Bampton Lecturer, it appears, reserves to himself the discretion to determine them for us on some future occasion.

In the latter part of his Lectures indeed, he, though under no misgiving, as he indignantly asserts, with regard to the effects of the sweeping principle propounded in the earlier part, guards the practical application of that principle by some important limitations. He tells us (p. 211) that "there are doctrines and practices which carry on their front convincing proof that they cannot have been revealed or commanded by God, and systems of religion which by this criterion may be shown to have sprung, not from divine appointment, but from human corruption;" in other words, that there is a point beyond which divine contradiction of human morality, or, in plain terms, divine immorality, cannot go. God cannot institute "licentious or inhuman rites of worship." Why? Because they are open to condemnation "for their regulative character, as contributing to the perpetual corruption of mankind" (p. 242). But as we know nothing of the Absolute Morality, how do we know that it excludes institutions which, according to ideas derived from human morality, have a bad "regulative" effect? Or how do we know that what the Lecturer here presumes to call the "perpetual corruption of mankind," is not really a perpetual elevation of man to a conformity with a higher morality than his own ?

An attempt is also made to draw a distinction between the " habitual observance of licentious or inhuman rites of worship " and " isolated facts, historically recorded as having been done by divine command, but not perpetuated in precepts for the imitation of posterity." But this distinction between bad precept and bad example is certainly not founded on anything in human morality, and it would be difficult to find a foundation for it in that " Absolute Morality" which is beyond the range of thought.

As Mr. Mansel's case stands at present, I maintain that there is no precept or example so foully licentious or so abominably inhuman, that if it is embodied in a religion professing to be attested by miracles we can affirm on grounds of morality that it is not from God.

In his letter to me, he throws no light upon these points. He does not supply any criterion by which, independently of miracles, we could accept the Founder of Christianity, and reject the Founders of Mormonism and Thuggee. But he produces a defence of his theory of a different and rather unexpected kind. He surprises us with the sudden announcement that it is not his own, but merely a " revival " and " repetition " of the theory put forth a century and a half ago by

Archbishop King and Bishop Browne. When propounded by those prelates, it was assailed, with an injustice equal to mine, by Berkeley : — *Bishop Berkeley*, Mr. Mansel always calls him ; but I think he is worthy by the loftiness and purity of his soul, if not by the mere power of his intellect to stand unmitred among the great. All this I ought to have known ; and it is pretty broadly intimated that I can save my "honesty" only by pleading guilty to culpable ignorance.

When Mr. Mansel wrote his Lectures, he was "fresh from the study of the above controversy," on the details of which he dwells with a solemnity calculated to invest it with the highest importance, pondering whether it was against Browne or King that a particular passage of Berkeley was directed ; and inclining, where the two differ, to agree with Browne rather than with King. He was "fully aware of all the hard things which had been said against the doctrine which he undertook to repeat." He knew that no less a man than Berkeley, besides "a host of other objectors," had denounced its original author "as an atheist or little better." Yet he "revived" and "repeated" it without giving his hearers or readers any warning against the terrible misconception to which, as he knew that it had once led, he must have known that it was liable again to lead. He launched upon the

Church, without any special safeguard, that which
Berkeley and a host of others had previously pro-
nounced to be atheism. This he now discloses, to
spring, as he thinks, a mine under me. But when
a controversialist keeps back a material part of his
case and afterwards produces it to confound an opponent, he is at the same time under the necessity
of explaining his previous reservation to the public.
Mr. Mansel's explanation to the public is that he
" did not anticipate for his lectures any great circu-
lation beyond the precincts of his own University";
and that in Oxford, though " Browne's name might
be little known," (I can assure him it is astonish-
ingly little known) he thought we must all be
perfectly familiar with Archbishop Whately's edition of King's Discourse on Predestination, and
the notes to Bishop Copleston's Discourses on the
same subject; books which are not to be found
in all our College libraries. Surely when the
Bampton Lectures had come to a third edition,
and had awakened cries of dissent and even of
horror, their author must have begun to suspect
that they had reached the outer world, and that the
outer world was unprovided with the necessary an-
tidote. Yet in the apologetic preface to the Third
Edition there is no mention of Browne, King, or
Berkeley; not a word of all this which is now put
forward as essential to a right understanding of the

question. Surely then I might pretty reasonably assume that Mr. Mansel's case was fairly before the world.

May it not even be said that some acknowledgment was due to Archbishop King and Bishop Browne, as the real authors of the theory by the " revival" and " repetition" of which Mr. Mansel was winning the fame of a second Butler. A critic in the *Rambler* accused the author of the Bampton Lectures, not without plausibility, of having borrowed the gist of his book without acknowledgment from the teaching of Dr. Newman. Mr. Mansel treated this accusation as " one of the most serious that could be brought against the character of an author," and met it by professing ignorance of Dr. Newman's works ; an ignorance which perhaps is at least as remarkable in an Oxford theologian and controversialist, as an ignorance of the works of Archbishop King and Bishop Browne, or even of Bishop Copleston's and Archbishop Whately's commentaries upon them.

We are not engaged in tracing the pedigree of Mr. Mansel's theories : we are engaged in examining their soundness. But I am convinced that even if we were tracing their pedigree we should merely mystify the question by suffering ourselves to be drawn off into the details of a controversy carried on at the beginning of the eighteenth

H

century between Anglican divines. Kant is Mr. Mansel's teacher. Kant, by his criticism of the speculative reason, was brought to the conclusion that there could be no proof of the existence of God, and that theology was impossible. The abyss of Atheism yawned before him. He started aside into a supplemental theory of a Divine Law of Morality and a Divine Lawgiver, apprehended not by our speculative, but by our practical reason. Where Kant started aside, Mr. Mansel went straight on. This is the true pedigree of the Bampton Lectures.

Mr. Mansel scornfully reproaches Kant for his inconsistency. Kant may have been inconsistent; but the inconsistency of such a man was worth studying. If Mr. Mansel had studied it, he might perhaps have found that Kant had been driven from his logical course, not by the sudden failure of his powerful intellect, but by the cry of his religious heart.

Had Kant's philosophy been presented to the Bampton Lecturer's admirers entire, it would not have been very cordially welcomed. But the sceptical part of it, without the religious part, is hailed as a new pillar added to the tottering edifice of the faith.

If we are to travel into the sources of the lectures, Sir William Hamilton will of course claim his part: though, without presuming to undertake

his defence, I can imagine that his other disciples
might put in certain demurrers on his behalf.
Some acknowledgment would also be due to Dr.
Hampden. But these are the antiquities of the
question: we are concerned with that which is
before us alone.

We cannot allow ourselves to be much influenced,
though it seems to be expected we shall, by the
spiritual authority of Archbishop King. He was a
high Tory and advocate of passive obedience, who
modified his previous convictions at the Revolution,
and, amidst the irreverent reflections of his former
friends, accepted a mitre from the usurping government; though he complains to his correspondent,
Swift, that "as he was an honest man, he had
courted the greatest Whigs, but never could get the
reputation of being counted one." He was long
among the most prominent and busy movers in the
element of Irish politics, where, I fear, in those days
he saw little but "morality with a human element"
to use his disciple's phrase. His principal work is
his " Treatise on the Origin of Evil," in which this
prelate of the Irish Establishment teaches us with
much unction to acquiesce in questionable arrange-
ments as the best which the circumstances of the
case permitted Providence to make; and proves
that the weaker classes of animals, as they could not
be allowed to exist on any other terms, may think

themselves comparatively happy in being eaten up
by the strong.

In such an age and country, and amidst such
associations, a writer may be forgiven for saying the
things which King said in his treatise on Predestination. He might be forgiven for saying (p. 13)[1]
that the qualities of mercy and love were no more
properly in God than hands and eyes; that the best
of men, St. Paul, for instance, had no more proper
notion of God's love and mercy than a blind man
had of colours (p. 18) : that if we know anything of
Him who is the highest object of our love, it must
be by deductions of reason, by analogy and comparison (p. 21). He might be forgiven for asserting (p. 21) that the knowledge given us of the Divine
Attributes by reason or Scripture was no higher
than the knowledge given us of a country by a map
which, being only paper and ink, diversified with
several strokes and lines, has in itself very little
likeness to earth, mountains, valleys, lakes, and
rivers, yet, by proportion and analogy, is undeniably
very instructive; for enjoining us (p. 34) to rest
satisfied with an arbitrary selection of objects of
mercy in God, as we do in a prince, " who of many
equal malefactors, reprieves one for an instance of
his mercy and *power*, and suffers the rest to be
carried to execution ;" for bidding us (p. 35) con-

[1] The references are to Whately's edition.

sider, as a reason for acquiescing in total ignorance of the real nature of God, "how many honour and obey their prince who never saw him, who never had any personal knowledge of him, *and could not distinguish him from another man if they should meet him*;" for asking (p. 42) whether a mere knowledge of effects without causes will not serve our practical purposes in the case of our religious affections as well as in the case of light or heat. He might be forgiven for holding (p. 36) that "we do not know any more of the person or nature of God but that He is our Creator and Governor," forgetting that He is our Father, and that in Him we live and move and have our being. All this might be forgiven in a prelate of the Irish Establishment at the beginning of the eighteenth century, though even in him it moved the indignation of a spiritual nature like that of Berkeley, and drew strong language from his gentle lips. But Mr. Mansel is not writing in the Irish Church at the beginning of the eighteenth century. He may "not think that the world has grown much wiser on the point in question" since that time : but he may rest assured that the world has opened some new questions, and that if he aspires to the character of a religious philosopher in the present age, he has other requirements to satisfy than any which were satisfied by the productions of Archbishop King.

I have read, at Mr. Mansel's suggestion, a part of the forgotten writings of Bishop Browne : and I can only profess my humble opinion that in this, as in most cases, oblivion has been just. As a fair specimen of the Bishop's philosophy, I will give the most important paragraph of the *Divine Analogy*, his most important work. The italics are his own.

"METAPHOR in general is a substitution of the *idea* or *conception* of one thing, with the term belonging to it, to *stand for* another thing, on account of an *appearing* similitude only, *without any real resemblance and true correspondency between the things compared;* as when the Psalmist describes the verdure and fruitfulness of valleys by *laughing* and *singing.* ANALOGY in general is the *substituting* the idea or *conception* of one thing to stand for and represent another on account of a *true resemblance and correspondent reality in the very nature of the things compared.* It is defined by Aristotle ἰσότης τοῦ λόγου, an *Equality or Parity of Reason*; though in strictness and truth the Parity of Reasoning is rather *built* on the similitude and analogy and consequent to them, than the same thing with them. (*Divine Analogy, p. 8.*)

Should any one be led to look again into the theory of these prelates and their followers, I would venture to suggest to him that the key to the whole is their assumption, which I cannot help thinking without foundation, that there is some special relation denoted by the term Analogy. The primary sense of the word in its original language is *proportion*, and I am convinced that where it is used by English philosophers to denote a special relation other than proportion, and made the ground of what is called *analogical* reasoning, there is no other idea at bottom than the common one of *resemblance*. King, for example, says that 'the Attributes of the Deity (Wisdom, Justice, &c.) are not to be regarded as the *same* with their human qualities which have the same names, but are called so by *resemblance* and *analogy* only'; clearly using *resemblance* and *analogy* as convertible terms, denoting the same relation. Butler also uses *analogy* and *likeness* indiscriminately. Archbishop Whately says that the courage of one man is only *analogous* to the courage of another man. What qualities, then, *resemble*, or are identical with, each other?

Butler, though he built his religious philosophy on *analogy*, and evidently attributed some special force to it, declined, rather strangely, to inquire wherein that force lay. I venture to think there is nothing special in his great argument. It is simply this, that God, being a perfectly consistent Being, may be expected to act towards us on the whole as he acts towards us in this present life, and to be to us in Revelation what He is in nature. The flaw, it would seem, is that the cases are not the same: an immortal soul being a different thing from a mortal life, and a Revelation which is intended to clear up Nature being a different thing from the Nature which it is intended to clear up.

The truth is that even *resemblance*, strictly speaking, is a relation which cannot exist between abstract qualities. They must be either the same or different. A particular quality may be present in different degrees in different beings, but wherever it is present it must, in its essence, be the same. The mental process of abstraction eliminates every thing but identity of essence.

If the moral qualities of the Deity and those of man are not allowed to be the same, the assumption that they 'resemble or 'correspond to each other,' either in the way of 'analogy' or in any other way, is utterly gratuitous and groundless. Bishop Copleston, in attempting to pull down the 'exalted pretensions' of man, has inadvertently pulled his own sacred edifice about his ears.

Let us attempt to draw out the supposed analogy in form. ' As the quality of justice is to human nature, so to the Divine nature is — what ? If we say ' Divine justice,' we are running round in a ridiculous circle. If we say 'some quality un-known,' how can we be assured that this unknown quality bears to any human quality the relation denoted by analogy ? And even if we could be assured of this, what light would it throw upon the question ?

If the term *analogous* is applied not to the relation between the two things themselves, but to the representation of one of them; supposing the re-presentation to be true, it is simply a true representation, and the term *analogous* is needless ; supposing the representation to be untrue, then, if it is tendered as true, it is a misrepresentation, and if it is not tendered as true, it is a mere counter or symbol. It is difficult to see what other case there can be.

To leave King and Browne and return to the point. Mr. Mansel has destroyed all connection between the morality of men and the morality of God, by laying it down that the morality of God is ' Absolute,' and proving that the *Absolute* and the *Infinite* " are, like the *Inconceivable* and the *Imperceptible*, names indicating, not an object of thought or consciousness at all, but the mere absence of the conditions under which consciousness is possible." This results from the general arguments of his book, an argument of which neither Browne nor King ever dreamed. And after coming distinctly to this conclusion, he undertakes to assure us (Bampton Lect., p. 208) that the " Absolute Morality" is uncreated and co-eternal with the Deity, and (p. 209) that there is a higher and unchangeable principle embodied in the forms of human morality, which he says " we have abundant reason to believe." We have all abundant reason to shrink from saying the contrary ; but it is a pity that we were not, out of the abundance, furnished with one reason for the belief. If reason is

I

capable of determining that human morality contains a partial embodiment of a principle which lies
utterly beyond the range of our thought and
consciousness, it will surely be difficult to confine
this presumptuous faculty within any assignable
bounds. To doubt that Absolute Morality is
eternal and uncreated, Mr. Mansel says "were
blasphemy." But he will perceive, on reflection,
that unless we can form a conception of God, we
shall never come to the point at which 'blasphemy'
can arise. We may say that to doubt the Eternity
of Morality is odious and inconvenient, but,
philosophically, we can say no more.

Besides this general argument, however, Mr.
Mansel proves that the Morality of man cannot be
the same with the Morality of God by a special
argument, which he "acquits me of intentional
unfairness" for not stating, when I expressly said
that what I was giving was his 'conclusion.'
Human Morality, he says, is a law imposed by a
lawgiver, but there can be no lawgiver to impose a
law on God; and this, he thinks, makes an essential
difference between the two moralities. In his own
words—" To human conception it seems impossible
that absolute morality should be manifested in the
form of a *law of obligation*; for such a law implies
relation and subjection to the authority of a lawgiver. And as all human morality is manifested in

this form, the conclusion seems unavoidable, that human morality, even in its highest elevation, is not identical with, nor adequate to measure, the Absolute Morality of God." But, in the first place, if we can know nothing of the Absolute Morality, we cannot know that it is not manifested in the form of a law. Hooker, in a passage which is at least as pertinent to a philosophical discussion as that which Mr. Mansel has quoted, speaks of " that law eternal which God Himself hath made to Himself. . . . . . that law the Author and *Observer* whereof is one only God to be blessed for ever." In the second place, how can the mere mode of injunction or imposition make a difference in the essence of the thing enjoined or imposed ? Does Mr. Mansel mean to affirm that God alters the nature of morality by bidding man to be moral ? If so, I do not see how he will escape from the inference that the nature of morality is altered every time it is imposed by a father on his son, and that the virtue practised by a good citizen is different in kind from the virtue inculcated by the State.

The school of Browne and King have another reason to give for maintaining that the human virtues cannot possibly be identical with the Divine. The human virtues they say are essentially the virtues of a Being in whom spirit is united with matter. In this they are followed by Bishop Copleston.

They and he might surely as well have said that human virtues were essentially the virtues of a biped.

Mr. Mansel must recollect that in his Bampton Lectures (p. 39) he has distinctly laid it down by implication that the attributes of God differ from those of men, not in degree only, but in *kind*. The supposition that they differ not in kind but only in degree, he condemns as " the method of the vulgar Rationalism." It is for him to harmonize this with what he says elsewhere about "a correspondence" and "a common principle," as well as with the possibility, which he would scarcely be prepared to exclude, of sympathy and communion between God and man.

I reminded Mr. Mansel that the Bible sets out with the declaration that man was created in the image of God. His reply is that " whatever may be the exact import of that declaration, as applied to Adam in Paradise, it should not be forgotten that the same book which tells us of man's creation in God's image tells us also of his fall from that image." But in what passage of the book of Genesis, or of any other book of Scripture, are we told that the moral nature of man fell from the image in which he was created in such a sense that his moral sentiments and qualities after the Fall became different in kind from his moral sentiments and qualities before the Fall. In what part of the Bible is any hint of this tremendous revolution in the moral world to be found ? Mr. Mansel had before made *two*, now he has made *three* moralities ;—the Divine, the Human before the Fall, and the Human after the Fall. Perhaps if he adopts certain theories as to the moral effects of Baptism, he may be led to add a *fourth* to the list. If this doctrine is not true, it surely almost deserves to be called portentous.

Mr. Mansel admits that the expression, "Moral Miracles," which he used to explain certain passages apparently opposed to morality in the Old Testament, is "open to a sneer.' Let us hope then that in a matter of such vital importance he will cease to propagate as true a doctrine which will not stand the fair test of ridicule. A preacher of his school has substituted the phrase "Moral Marvels :" but unfortunately the use of soft names does not soften the things, while it awkwardly suggests that the things require softening. I repeat that, if the morality of God is different from that of man, there is no need of "Moral Miracles " or "Moral Marvels," or any other device to explain the divergence of the two moralities in any particular instance. Acts which to man are immoral may be, and in some cases must be, normal and habitual acts of God.

I find difficulty in believing that a man of Mr. Mansel's acuteness can really suppose that because I think his method of defending the morality of

certain acts open to ridicule, I must have fallen
into an undesigned coincidence with Tindal, who
holds the acts themselves to have been immoral.
The dreadful figment of the two moralities
(I may speak of it in plain language since Mr.
Mansel was not its originator) has been adopted
mainly to prevent men from questioning certain
supposed instances of questionable morality in the
Old Testament. But I cannot help asking those
in whose province this matter lies, whether we
may not hope to solve these difficulties without
the use of an expedient which would overturn
religion and the moral world, if only two things
are borne in mind (1.) that the Jewish nation
was a nation, not a miracle, and that it had a
history parallel to the histories of other nations,
though pervaded by a higher spiritual life, and
(2.) that while the essence of morality and of
the moral character, which is the love of our
neighbour, is unchanging, the moral code depending on our known relation to other men changes
and improves as the moral vision of man extends
with the progress of enlightenment and civilization,
from his family to his tribe, from his tribe to his
nation, from his nation to his kind. Men may,
without a breach of morality, repeat the destruction
of the Canaanites if they can dissolve the great
community of the human race, and put themselves

back into the primitive age of war and conquest;
and they will then find that to hold the land
they have conquered by the title of a purer religion and a purer morality is at least better than
to hold it by a genealogy or by the spear. They
may applaud the slaying of another Sisera, if they
can put themselves back into the age of exclusive
patriotism ; and they will then find that exclusive
devotion to a country, whose God is Jehovah,
is more elevating than exclusive devotion to a
country whose God is Jupiter or Baal. They
may revive the Jewish slave-law if they can put
themselves back into the era of universal slavery;
and they will then find the Jewish slave-law a
great improvement in humanity on the slave-laws
of other nations. They may restore the Jewish
parent's power over the life of his child, if they
can put themselves back into the age when personal rights, and the rights of the state, as against
the family, were but half understood, and they
will then find that the Jewish rule on this subject
was at least far better then the secret and uncontrolled
exercise of the *patria potestas* in the much later
and generally more civilized age of Rome. If
indeed an instance of a retrograde tendency in
matters affecting the moral code could be detected
in the Old Testament, and proved to be an essential
part of the Dispensation, the case would no doubt

become serious. But I am not aware that any such instance has been yet produced.

It appears to me also, I confess, that what objectors commonly point out as discrepancies of doctrine in the Old Testament are in fact merely instances of a gradual spiritual elevation, such as we must have expected to find, unless it had been the design of Providence entirely to exempt the Jewish nation from all spiritual effort, and to make their religious history an automatic exhibition utterly disconnected with the general " travailing " of humanity and alien to the sympathies of mankind.

If we find what we think malevolent sentiments attributed to a Beneficent Being in the Old Testament, and are tempted on that account to frame any peculiar theory respecting the Divine morality, the first thing will be to inquire whether the sentiments are really malevolent. Hatred of evil, for instance, as distinguished from hatred of the evil doer, is not really a malevolent but a benevolent sentiment, as it tends to remove what is odious from the character of another.[1]

One who has been represented as unconsciously coinciding with Tindal, may be excused for offering these remarks which, at least, show that he does not take Tindal's view of the subject.

[1] There is an excellent treatise on the *Malevolent Sentiments*, by Hey, privately printed, which well deserves to be published. It goes more into the Scriptural question than his four published sermons on the same subject.

The philosophy of history, if it is treated as an enemy by the defenders of Christianity, will prove a deadly one; but if it is received in the spirit proper to those who have absolute faith in the God of Truth, it may after all prove no enemy but a powerful friend.

I will not attempt to go into the distinction between " the immutability of the moral *principles,*" and " the immutability of the *acts* in which those principles are manifested in practice," by which Mr. Mansel (Bamp. Lect. p. 206, and Pref. to Third Ed. p. xvii.) apparently wishes to reconcile his theory of the two moralities with the doctrine of Immutable Morality, having, perhaps, the fear of Cudworth before his eyes. What he means by a mutable or immutable *act*, I do not pretend to understand. Acts and their circumstances are of course infinitely mutable and various. But by no possible variation or permutation of acts can we conjure away the difficulty regarding the principle. If morality is immutable, there cannot be two moralities: and if there are two moralities, morality cannot be immutable.

Elsewhere, (Lect. p. 208) Mr. Mansel has spoken of man as placed by his Maker in circumstances " by which *the eternal principles of right and wrong* are *modified* in relation to this present life." That which is *modified* is changed; and

K

if the eternal principles of right and wrong are
changed, under any circumstances whatever, morality is not immutable. It concerns the author
of a religious philosophy very deeply to come to a
clear conclusion, and to use unwavering language
on this point.

If man is here placed "in circumstances by which
the eternal principles of right and wrong are modified in relation to this present life," it is difficult to
suppress the reflection that this life must be a very
equivocal preparation for the next: at least, if in
the next life, we are destined to encounter the
eternal principles of right and wrong in their un-
modified form.

" We are indeed bound to believe that a Revelation given by God can never contain any thing
that is *really* unwise or unrighteous ; but we are
not always capable of estimating exactly the wisdom
or righteousness of particular doctrines or precepts."
(Bamp. Lect. p. 240). These words, which are
from the last and the most mature of the Lectures,
will, I believe, be found, on attentive consideration,
plainly to imply that the difference between the
human and the Divine Morality maintained in
earlier lectures is not *real :* and that all the Divine
Acts must be ultimately reconcilable with a wisdom
and a righteousness which are, in kind, identical
with ours.

But as Mr. Mansel thus admits that no Revelation given by God (and of course no other manifestation of His nature) can contain any thing really unwise or unrighteous, he will do well either to modify or very carefully to guard a passage in the preface to his third edition, (p. xiii.) where he states that "it is useless, were it possible, to disguise that the representation of God after the highest human morality which we are capable of conceiving, is not sufficient to account for all the phenomena exhibited by the course of His natural Providence." For these words are a relapse into the theory of the two moralities. The suggestion they convey is that in the Providence, and of course in the Nature of the Deity, there are contradictions of Morality and Justice which it is useless, if it were possible, to disguise.

There are parts of the Creator's government which we are not able at once to reconcile with the beneficence and the justice which He has implanted in our hearts, and of which we cannot choose but regard Him as the archetype. To admit this is one thing. It is another thing to pronounce, and believe it pious to pronounce, that reconciliation is hopeless, or that we are not to use the reason He has given us in endeavouring to effect it. The difficulties mentioned by Mr. Mansel in the passage to which I have just referred are the infliction of physical suffering, the permission of moral evil, the adversity of the good, the prosperity of the wicked, the crimes of the guilty involving the misery of the innocent, the tardy appearance and partial distribution of moral and religious knowledge in the world. Now these facts are difficulties it is true, but they do not present an adamantine resistance—on the contrary, they yield and yield considerably—to the efforts of our moral reason. They have yielded more to those efforts in the proportion as the moral reason of man has been improved by the extension of his knowledge, the exercise of his faculties, and the refinement of his heart; and metaphysicians will be limiting not only religious thought, but Providence, if they lay it down as certain that what has yielded so far can never yield any further. As to physical pain, we can discern that it is a widely different thing from moral evil, and that in fact it is to a great extent productive of moral good. As to moral evil, we can discern that if there were no obstacle for the soul to contend against, there could not be that moral excellence which is the result of effort, and which is the highest good conceivable by our minds. The adversity of the good and the prosperity of the wicked are difficulties of which the ordinary sense of man relieves itself by assuming that God is, in an intelligible sense, just, and will redress hereafter all that is unjust here; though by proving metaphysically that God is not, in an intelligible sense, just, we shall bring them back upon ourselves. The difficulty presented by "the crimes of the guilty involving the misery of the innocent" admits of a similar solution for the believers in a single morality; since, if the moral nature of God is identical with ours, we may be sure He will not allow any man, in the end, to suffer by any crimes but his own. The difficulty which stands last in the list—"the tardy appearance and partial distribution of moral and religious knowledge in the world" —is a terrible difficulty indeed. I believe, if there were no other philosophy than that of the Bampton Lectures, it would overwhelm the heart of man with darkness and despair. But just as, from the great awakening of speculation and the extension of our sympathies beyond the pale of Christendom to the whole human race, this difficulty begins to press severely upon us, there arises, to countervail it, the healing conviction that the community of mankind is a community indeed, and that what is given to one member of it is, though as yet we know not how, given to all.

Why should we think that the way to a solution of these mysteries is inexorably closed, or that our efforts to solve them, if made in the sincerity of our hearts, are offences against God? If the relation between God and man is one of affection, it is quite natural (according to all we know or can imagine of such relations) that our knowledge of the Divine Goodness should not be given to us at once, without exertion on our part, or without the interposition of difficulties and contrary appearances at the outset, which we may be permitted, in some measure at least, ultimately to pierce through. For it is under these and not under the opposite conditions that affection, as we experience it, is best formed and becomes most intense and deep. These new doubts and misgivings which arise from time to time, with the progress of the world, as man's moral sensibility becomes keener, his vision more enlarged, and his speculative powers more active, may after all be intended as a school of mixed intellectual and moral effort by which we shall be taught more deeply to appreciate and more intensely to love the Divine Perfection. At all events those who pronounce that it is not so, prior to the ultimate disclosure of God's purposes, might, I think, be charged with constructing an *a priori* scheme for the government of the world ; which is thought by the school of philosophers, against whom I am arguing, a sufficient rebuff to man whenever he asks for an explanation of his difficulties and an assurance of the truth.

There are indeed difficulties arising not out of

the nature of things, or the plain sense of Christianity, but out of technical theology, such as the difficulties of Predestination dealt with in the treatise of Archbishop King, which, as they are the mere offspring of human folly, dogmatism, and arrogance, it is not to be expected that Providence will enable reason to solve. But men of sense will scarcely allow that the way out of these difficulties is to be found by tampering with the immutability of morals and inventing a peculiar morality for God.

That we shall never in this world know as fully as we are known is certain : but it does not follow that we cannot attain real knowledge, or that the boundaries of the knowledge attainable by us have as yet been seen. The limits of human reason must be fixed not by the clergy of any persuasion but by the will of Providence : and what the limits fixed by Providence may be, can be learned only by conscientiously exerting reason to the utmost on all subjects, and especially on those which most deeply concern us as moral and religious beings. Where reason fails, for the time or finally, in matters of religion, there, for the time or finally, are fixed the limits of religious thought.

" But,' asks Mr. Mansel, if not 'identical with,' is human morality ' adequate to measure ' that of

God." And he desires to know definitely what is
meant by " measuring the morality of God." His
readers will probably suppose that the phrase is mine,
or at least that I have accepted it. The phrase is
his : I have not accepted it : I repudiate it as inappro-
priate, and as unfairly prejudicing the case of those
into whose mouths it is gratuitously put. It suggests
the presumptuous idea that man is morally on a level
with his Maker and competent to sit in judgment on
the Divine conduct. But no such idea is implied in
the assertion that human morality is identical with
divine, and that we are able, in virtue of that identity, to discern what does and what does not emanate
from a divine source. A child may be well assured
that a missive enjoining it to commit an act of
wickedness does not come from the father who has
trained it up in virtue; but it would be a very
strange mode of expression to say that in repudiating such a missive, the child assumed its moral
judgment to be " adequate to measure " the moral
judgment of its father. If a doctrine or precept be
contradictory to my moral nature, and subversive of
my moral life, 1 am not only competent but compelled to pronounce that it does not emanate from
the Author of my moral being. I shall therefore
reject it. But in so doing, be it observed, I shall
not be rejecting a Divine command. I shall only
be rejecting the human testimony on which the

assertion that the command is Divine is, in each case, necessarily founded. If I were to hear a voice from Heaven ordering me to commit an atrocious act of wickedness, I should no doubt be cast into fearful perplexity. But if another man tells me that he has heard, or that he has been informed that a third person has heard, a voice from Heaven ordering me to do such an act, I shall be in no perplexity at all. I shall simply conclude the witness, according to his general character, to be either mendacious or mistaken.

I must once more remind Mr. Mansel that what he has maintained, is not only the immeasurable and overwhelming difference in *degree* which we all feel must exist between the Divine attributes and human qualities, but a difference in *kind*. His theory not only humbles and abases man; it cuts him off morally from God.

In this part of Mr. Mansel's letter I note a passage which shows, I venture to think, that if my "general axiom" is "wanting in definiteness," his is capable of being made more clear. He supposes two men set to deal with a Scriptural difficulty, one pious, the other impious. The impious man applies to it his moral reason, after the method of Rational Religion. The pious man says "I am not able to judge by this criterion: there may be facts, of which I am ignorant, which, if I knew

L

them, might show the apparent injustice to be really just: or there may be other attributes of God, whose action I can but imperfectly understand, which, if I understood them better, might perhaps explain this apparent anomaly." When " ignorance of facts" is imported into the case, the question is put upon an entirely new footing. Ignorance of facts is a widely different thing from the want of moral sympathy, and of the corresponding power of moral appreciation. That it is necessary to know all the facts of a case before we can form a moral judgment on it, whether in matters human or Divine, is a position which no one will venture to impugn. But this was not the position which Mr. Mansel set out to prove against the advocates of Rational Religion, in eight highly abstruse and metaphysical Lectures on the Limits of Religious Thought.

No one is unwilling to admit that there are mysteries in the Divine Government which, from our ignorance of the general plan of Creation, will never be cleared up to our understandings while we remain upon earth. What we are so unwilling to admit is, that there are things in the Divine Government clear to our understandings, but repugnant to our moral sense.

Mr. Mansel relapses into the theory of the two moralities when after *ignorance of facts* he introduces, in somewhat strange juxtaposition, " other attributes of God " : for a moral nature with other attributes would of course be a different moral nature. But he returns to the theory of a single morality, when he calls an appearance of injustice in God an " anomaly" : for if the Divine and human moralities were different, their divergence in any given case would be no " anomaly" at all.

The " moral miracles" which Mr. Mansel has introduced, must of course take their place beside the physical miracles, as evidences of religion. I believe it will appear that, according to Mr. Mansel's theory, they are the only moral evidences left. To treat any one of these as an " anomaly," and explain it away, would be to explain away one of the evidences of religion.

In the words of the Lord's Prayer, "Forgive us our trespasses, as we forgive them that trespass against us," it seems to be clearly implied that there is a sympathy in regard to the act of free forgiveness between the Divine Nature and the human, to which we are permitted to appeal. Some astonishment therefore was created among the readers of Mr. Mansel's book by the assertion that " it is obvious on a moment's reflection, that the duty of man to forgive the trespasses of his neighbour rests precisely upon those features of human nature which cannot by any analogy be regarded as representing an image of God." I think there is here an irreconcilable contradiction ; and I regard that contradiction as a decisive and welcome proof, that the theory of religion, and of the relations between God and man propounded in the Bampton Lectures is not identical with the Christian Faith. In his present Letter, Mr. Mansel says nothing which in any degree shakes or even touches this conviction : and I must decline to enter into a discussion, which I cannot regard as relevant, as to the doctrine of Atonement and the views held on that subject by Priestley, or by Clarke. I will only observe in passing, that if in stating my general principle, I have adopted Clarke's words, it was simply because they were the best. I have not "appealed to Clarke's authority," nor do I desire in any way to shelter myself beneath it. Mr. Mansel admonishes me that "it is dangerous to borrow the weapons of a great metaphysician, without first becoming acquainted with the manner in which he wields them." I bow to the just consciousness of superior learning which reveals itself in this admonition, and I will remember the warning whenever I need "weapons." But for the present purpose I need none. The same phrase occurred in the Bampton Lectures ; and it recals to my mind certain passages touching the usefulness of particular lines of argument to the good cause, where the writer appears to me to ignore obligations which I recognise, and to recognise obligations which I ignore.

I will venture to add, in reference not only to this, but to other passages in Mr. Mansel's Letter, that while, as I sincerely believe, he cannot possibly presume too much on his own learning, he may possibly be led to presume too much on the general ignorance. In such an age as this, many men who are not professional theologians, are compelled to read, for practical purposes, books which they would otherwise have let alone. They do not thereby become learned : but they do become less liable to be daunted by a display of erudition, or baffled by mystification ; and they are emboldened to apply the rough test of common sense to doctrines which are intended to affect their practical belief and life.

I pointed out to Mr. Mansel, in my previous remarks, that by denying the identity of Human and Divine Morality, he had cut away all arguments for the Immortality of the Soul which are founded on our faith in Divine Justice : for if we know nothing of the Absolute Justice of the Deity, or if we know that it is not identical with our Justice, there can be no ground for presuming that it will lead Him to redress the sufferings of the good in a future state of existence. On this

point, at all events, I should have thought Mr.
Mansel would have felt himself bound to give
a satisfactory explanation in his own name. Such
however is not the case. All he has to say is
this—

To another remark of yours—" If we know nothing of the Absolute
Justice of God, what presumption is there that it will lead Him to redress
the sufferings of the good in a future state of existence?"—I am almost
tempted to reply, with Bishop Copleston, "when this author asks,
'How can men know that they shall be rewarded or punished in a
future state, but from the consideration of God's justice,' I answer
confidently, We know it from the Scriptures, and we could know it in
no other way." At any rate, I believe that, had the Christian Revelation not been given, men's "presumptions" on this point would be
now, after eighteen centuries, as dark and doubtful as they were before
that Revelation came. And when, even in this nineteenth century, I
see one disciple of an advanced school of progress arguing that the
human soul, as having a beginning and a development, must necessarily
also have an end; when I find another assuring me that the belief in
the remedy of wrongs in a future life is a great hindrance to repentance
and amendment in this life; when a third asserts that the belief in a
true death, which completely ends the life of the individual, can alone
render man capable of true religion and self-denial; when a fourth pro-
claims that the last enemy that shall be destroyed by Criticism is the
belief in a future existence; when a fifth teaches that individual existence is the error from which it should be the aim of life to extricate
ourselves; and a sixth boasts of the moral superiority of a subjective
immortality in the minds of others, over the old objective immortality
which is radically selfish;—I am thankful that God has not left men,
even in this enlightened age, to grope after their future destiny by the
feeble rays of their unassisted reason, whether speculative or moral.

In his Bampton Lectures, Mr. Mansel, having
laid prostrate a party of Rationalists, raises over
them the triumphant shout, "These be thy Gods,
O Philosophy; these are the Metaphysics of Salvation!" I am almost tempted here to cry, though

in a less jubilant tone, This is orthodoxy! I point out to a great orthodox controversialist that he is clearly cutting away one of the main proofs of the immortality of the soul. He does not deny it. He gives not one word of explanation. He is content to tell us, in effect, that one Bishop and six sceptical philosophers have talked loosely on the subject. And then he turns the matter off with a sneer at "this enlightened age," as though the light of the world had been turned to moral darkness when the thoughts and aspirations of men passed beyond the philosophy of Bishop Copleston and Archbishop King.

I confess that I am neither overwhelmed nor surprised at the combination of testimony, from apparently opposite quarters, which Mr. Mansel here produces against the natural doctrine of the immortality of the soul. When Rational Religion is to be assailed, there is nothing very startling in finding an Anglican prelate arrayed on the same side with Feuerbach and Comte. By Mr. Mansel's account of his seven supporters, it appears that the Bishop is the most hopeless sceptic of the number. The rest have their difficulties and perplexities; some of them, by the way, capable of very easy removal, as, for instance, those arising out of the false notion that the Christian immortality is "individual and selfish." But they have still in

them that which is the root of belief, a faith in
the indications of their own spiritual nature. The
Bishop alone "confidently" contradicts the voice
of his own soul. Mr. Mansel is "almost tempted"
to follow the Bishop. I conjure him to pause, and
even to reconsider his own theory before he yields
to the temptation.

I would not willingly believe that Bishop Copleston, who, I have no doubt, was orthodox on
matters of less practical moment, was heterodox on
the immortality of the soul. Before concluding
that he was so, I should at least like to know that
the case was fairly put before him. It may be
granted that we are unable to distinguish the spirit
from the body in the compound man, or to pronounce, by actual observation, that when the bodily
part dies the spiritual part survives. The result of
Butler's attempt to offer proof of this kind is one
among many warnings against relying indiscriminately on all that has been written by a great man.
But though we cannot actually distinguish the soul
from the body, we may be sure that our moral life
is the essence of our being, and that our moral life
does not end when the body dies. We may be sure
of this, at least, unless our whole nature is a lie. If
a single man can be found, whose consciousness,
fairly interrogated, tells him, or suffers him to act on
the belief, that the death of the body closes the moral

account, and that when he is dead it will be all the same for him whether in his life he has done good or evil, I may think it possible to believe that there is no proof, except in Scripture, of the immortality of the soul. But when the evidence of Scripture alone is left, perhaps it will be found not to be quite so explicit as is assumed. The Old Testament, according to the view of the acute Warburton, contains no revelation on the subject: and the Gospel rather grounds its announcements of future rewards and punishments on a conviction of the immortality of the soul which it supposes already subsisting, and which it ratifies, than reveals that doctrine in express terms.

Together with the natural proofs of the immortality of the soul, arising from our faith in Divine Justice, Mr. Mansel's theory destroys the natural proof of a Wise and Beneficent Creator. The only Wisdom and Beneficence which we can discern in Creation, or by any possibility recognize, are a Wisdom and Beneficence consisting, like our own, in the right adaptation of means to good ends. And it would seem impossible to identify these with the Attributes of a Being of whose Moral Nature we can know absolutely nothing, or if we can know anything, can know only that it is different in kind from ours. For any sense, therefore, that the terms Creative Wisdom and Beneficence convey to our

M

understanding, we might as well say that the
Universe is filled with marks of Malevolence and
Folly. Paley's Evidences, the Bridgewater Trea-
tises, and all works of that description, must be
thrown aside as being mere tissues of talk about
that which it was metaphysically impossible that
the writers should apprehend. So in fact must all
works on Natural Theology except the Bampton
Lectures for 1858, which will be preserved to prove
to us that Natural Theology does not exist.

Mr. Mansel in his Lectures, (p. 144) speaking
of our power of apprehending the Deity, used the
expression " we behold effects only and not causes."
I took the natural import of this expression to be,
that we are cognizant of Creation (I should rather
have said of the World) only, not of a Creator:
and I observed, with immediate, but not with exclusive reference to this particular passage, that it is
to blank materialism and empiricism that such
reasonings inevitably lead. That such reasonings
do, as a matter of fact, lead to empiricism and
materialism, Mr. Mansel can hardly doubt, since
the main doctrine of his Lectures has been adopted
in his own words by a very able man, as the
foundation of what he and I should agree in
calling a great empirical and materialistic system.[1]

[1] Mr. Herbert Spencer (of whose honesty and ability as a writer, I
desire to speak with the most sincere respect,) would himself say that
his system was neither materialist nor spiritualist. But he could
hardly say that it was not empirical, and it certainly excludes God.

Whether the particular words, " we behold effects only, not causes," ought to tend to empiricism and materialism, is a question the answer to which depends on the exact import of the words. Taken literally, they would of course be unmeaning, since the two terms effect and cause are strictly correlative, and the two ideas inseparable from each other; so that we cannot apprehend a thing as an effect without, in the same act of thought, apprehending another thing as its cause. But the obvious meaning of the words is, that we apprehend phenomena merely, without apprehending any cause: and if this is not empiricism and materialism, it is difficult to say what is.

Mr. Mansel asks me whether I am prepared to say that we actually do behold the creative mind in the act of creation, as we are conscious of our own deliberations and determinations in the production of our own acts? I answer that this is not what I affirmed, nor what he apparently denied. He seems to allow that we may "know the movements of God's mind in Creation," though not "by direct perception, as we know the modes of our own mind," yet "by inference or conjecture as we infer or conjecture the thoughts and feelings of our neighbours." Is this his explanation of beholding effects without beholding causes? If so, his doctrine is indeed a most harmless one;

but by admitting that we are as cognizant of the relation between the Divine Acts and the Divine Nature as we are cognizant of the relation between the acts and nature of each other, he puts his own theory out of court.

"The invisible things of Him from the Creation of the World are clearly seen, being understood by the things that are made, even His Eternal Power and Godhead"—I think the statement that "we behold effects not causes" requires explanation to bring it into accordance with these words.

Mr. Mansel says that this statement of his is a mere repetition of a passage in Butler's Sermon on the Ignorance of Man ; and this he evidently thinks must put an end to the question. It is precisely in reference to a citation of Butler that he has laid down the salutary principle, which cannot be too often repeated, that "it is of little importance by what authority an opinion is sanctioned, if it will not itself bear the test of sound criticism." The Sermon on the Ignorance of Man is at least half rhetorical. The passage on which Mr. Mansel relies is "Creation is absolutely and entirely out of our depth, and beyond the extent of our utmost reach. And yet it is *as certain that God made the World,* as it is certain that *effects must have a cause.* It is indeed *in general* no more than effects that the most knowing

are acquainted with ; for as to causes, they are
as entirely in the dark as the most ignorant."
This passage does not go, even verbally, the
length of Mr. Mansel's sweeping proposition, that
"we behold effects only, and not causes." It
implicitly admits that we are sometimes, though
not in general, acquainted with the causes of
things, and above all that the world certainly
discloses to us the First Cause, God. But the
train of thought to which it really belongs will
be best seen by viewing it in conjunction with
another passage in the same Sermon : — " Thus
the scheme of Providence, the ways and works
of God, are too vast, of too large extent for our
capacities. There is, as I may speak, such an
expanse of power and wisdom, and goodness, in
the formation and government of the world, as is
too much for us to take in or comprehend. Power
and wisdom, and goodness, are manifest to us in
all these works of God, which come within our
view : but there are likewise infinite stores of
each poured forth through the immensity of the
Creation ; no part of which can be thoroughly
understood, without taking in its reference and
respect to the whole : and this is what we have
not faculties for." Who has controverted the
justice of such sentiments as these ?

Butler depicted, in strong and eloquent language,

the inability of man's scientific intellect to take
in the designs of the Creator and the universal
order of creation. Perhaps if he were living at
the present day he would add some qualifying
words even on this point, in acknowledgment of
the vast scientific revelations which it has pleased
the Creator to make to man. Great things have
happened since his time. However, it is a wide
step from saying that we are in a state of great uncertainty as to the causes of physical phenomena, to
saying that we are in a state of total uncertainty as
to the moral nature of the Deity, and all that depends
upon it. Let the philosopher try the question by
the test of his own consciousness, as he easily may.
It gives no shock to our being to be assured that
the physical constitution of the world, and of our
bodies, will be changed like a vesture, necessary as
that constitution may be to the functions of our
present life, and certain as may be the wisdom of
the Creator in adapting it to those functions. It
would give no shock to our being, though it might
perplex our understandings, to be assured that in
another state of existence the laws of figures and
numbers would no longer hold good ; that two sides
of a triangle would be together less than the third
side, and that two and two would make five. But
let us once be assured that there is no certainty or
permanency in the truths of our moral nature ; that,

in another state, what is here vice may be virtue,
and what is here virtue may be vice ; that the moral
world, like the natural, is but a garment that shall
pass away; and our being will at once receive a
fatal shock, the heart of our moral nature will cease
to beat.

It is difficult to imagine anything less profitable
than the inquiry whether Butler does or does not
coincide, really or apparently, on any particular
point with a religious philosophy of which the main
element is Kantian criticism, and which, as a whole,
was so entirely beyond his anticipation. I should
think it very frivolous, in combating Mr. Mansel's
new theory that our highest knowledge is not speculative but regulative, to cite Butler's statement in
his sermon on the Love of God, that "Mankind
have a faculty by which they discern speculative
truth ;" or to meet the new doctrine of the difference
between Divine and human morality, by reminding
its propounder that Hooker speaks of the angels as
"seeing in God that character which is nowhere but
in themselves and us resembled," and that South,
in his sermon on *The Creation of Man in the Image
of God*, discards one explanation of the Fall as
inconsistent with the equity of God, and adopts
another explanation as more consistent with it,
clearly identifying the equity of God with the
equity of man, and making man "adequate to

measure " the equity of God. These writers were
not cognizant of the present question. It might be
more to the purpose to ask whether religious philosophy with all its voices, whether of the past or of
the present, does not cry out against a theory which
cuts man off from moral sympathy with God.

One word on the authority of Butler. I have
lived in a University where he is worshipped
almost as a fetish ; on which his authority has
weighed like an incubus ; and where, through
the weak side of his system, he has become
the unhappy parent of a pedagogic philosophy
which is always rapping people on the knuckles
with the ferule of " analogous difficulties," instead of trying to solve the doubts and satisfy
the moral instincts of mankind. Yet I would not
willingly yield to any one in rendering him that
free and rational homage which alone would be
acceptable to his greatness ; for men of his mark
do not care, either in the political or intellectual
world, to reign over slaves. In dry intellect he
was mighty, and in the annals of moral science his
name will no doubt be memorable for ever ; but
he was wanting in feeling and the power of sympathy, and his religious philosophy is grievously
marked with this defect. He could even commit
the cruel platitude of pointing to the waste of
seeds as a parallel to the waste of souls. We

know, unfortunately, almost as little of his life as we know of the life of Shakespeare; and we cannot tell exactly what it was in him that gave rise to his partiality for Roman Catholic ceremonialism: but we may be sure that the audacious scepticism of his age must have produced in his mind a strong reaction towards the sidé of awe, and a tendency rather to rebuke human presumption, than to cheer human effort, enter into human perplexities, and console human weakness. Coleridge approached the great questions touching man's estate with less power indeed, and less soundness of understanding, but with an ampler and deeper nature, with a more entire humanity. And Coleridge, rather than Butler, has been the anchor by which the religious intellect of England has ridden out, so far as it has ridden out, the storms of this tempestuous age.

Mr. Mansel concludes the preface to his Bampton Lectures by solemnly assuring Oxford of his conviction " that religious philosophy will flourish or fade within her walls, according as she perseveres or neglects to study the works and cultivate the spirit of her great son and teacher, Bishop Butler."[1] I, for one, demur to the worship of local idols in

---

[1] We are all in the habit of speaking of ourselves as a university in the third person feminine. But the members of Convocation collectively do not constitute a goddess. Assuredly they did not in the time of "her great son and teacher, Bishop Butler."

N

philosophy, even when recommended by the highest local authority, By people beyond "our walls," the University will be told in rude language that if she chooses thus to wrap herself up in her own productions, her narrow self-complacency will be justly punished by forfeiting the allegiance of the intellectual world. They counsel her ill for her greatness who bid her always rest satisfied with herself. They counsel her ill even for her safety who bid her bind herself to the stake of a philosophy now half obsolete in the middle of a rising tide.

Closely connected with Mr. Mansel's theory of the two different moralities, and indeed a part of the same structure, is his theory of Regulative Representations. The Divine morality being different from the human, it follows that no speculative knowledge, that is, in plain English, no real knowledge of God's Moral nature be given to man either through reason or by Revelation. God "has given us truths which are designed to be regulative rather than speculative; intended, not to satisfy our reason, but to guide our practice; not to tell us what God is in His absolute nature, but how He wills that we should think of Him in our present finite state." I venture to ask those religious persons, who may have exulted in Mr. Mansel's destruction of Rational Religion, to consider these words. They import, as it seems to me, no less than this; that the Manifestations of the Divine Nature to us, which form the ground of all religion, are not real manifestations but mere rules of thought and feeling imposed by a Supreme Will. It is of that will alone and of its pressure upon us that we are really conscious. Now, we may be compelled by power, contrary to the instincts of our moral nature, to say that we think in a particular manner, though we have no assurance that the thing actually is so : but mere will can scarcely command the real obedience even of our thoughts, much less of our affections. Affection can be moved by nothing but the presence of a real object; and if the essence of religion is the love of God, the·Bampton Lecturer, with the sword of a principle borrowed from Kant, has destroyed the essence of Religion, He has destroyed Revealed Religion as well as Natural, for the Kantian principle sweeps away both. The representation of God in the Bible, as well as that in nature and the heart of man, becomes a mere phantasmagoria ; at least we cannot know that it is more. Mr. Mansel indeed assures us (Lect. p. 145) that "the conceptions which we are *compelled* to adopt as the guides of our thoughts and actions now, may indeed, in the sight of a higher Intelligence, be but partial truth, but cannot be *total falsehood;*" just as he has in

mercy assured us that "there is a higher and
unchangeable principle embodied" in the "forms"
of "human morality." But both these momentous
assurances are left to rest on his own authority
alone. And even if they can be relied on as
authentic, their vagueness renders them practically
of little value. As I before ventured to intimate,
we shall scarcely be able to regard the Deity as
an object of affection, unless we can be assured not
only that there is a reality in the representations,
but which is the reality and which is the mask.

Mr. Mansel himself, indeed, appears to be of
opinion that any assurance of the truth is needless.
"We cannot say," he tells us, (p. 146) "that our
conception of the Divine Nature exactly resembles
that Nature in its absolute existence; for we know
not what that absolute existence is. But, for the
same reason, we are equally unable to say that it
does not resemble; for, if we know not the
Absolute and Infinite at all, we cannot say how far
it is or is not capable of likeness or unlikeness to
the Relative and Finite. We must remain content
with the belief that we have that knowledge of God
which is best adapted to our wants and training.
How far that knowledge represents God as He is,
we know not and we have no need to know." Man
has no need of Divine Truth: he has no need of a
real knowledge of God's Nature to guide him in

his endeavours to conform himself to the likeness of God!

"The *highest principles of thought and action* to which we can attain, are *regulative*, not *speculative :* they do not serve to satisfy the reason, but to guide the conduct : they do not tell us what things are in themselves, but how we must conduct ourselves in relation to them." If this be the case, it only remains for the philosopher to explain the source of a universal and most pernicious illusion. How came man to imagine that he had a reason, and that his conscience commanded him to use it to the best of his power on all subjects affecting his being, and especially on the highest ?

I ask again—and certainly without the slightest approach to a " sneer"—whether the Church of England, which is disposed to be so severe on heresies little affecting the core of our religion, is prepared to accept the doctrine that the Apostles beheld in their Master nothing but a " regulative representation," " not totally false,"[1] of the Divine Nature ? I refer of course to the Manifestation of Moral Perfection and of Divine sympathy with man. Not the most distant allusion was made by me to the Mystery of the Union of the Two Natures ; and if the reproach of irreverence attaches

---

[1] Mr. Mansel seems to forget that the expression " not totally false," is his own.

to those who have introduced that subject, it is not upon me that it can justly fall.

The sanctity which belongs to Divine things does not extend to the theories of a writer concerning them ; though, unfortunately, it is impossible to discuss the theories intelligibly without introducing the names of the things.

It has occurred to me occasionally in reading the Bampton Lectures, that the point to which I last adverted was not present at the time to the Lecturer's mind ; that he was reasoning about Revelation as though it were simply a series of theological propositions to be submissively accepted by the human understanding, and overlooking, for the moment, the manifestation of the Divine Nature in the person of our Lord, as well as the communion between the soul and its Maker.

Some divines are apt to place the Almighty under strange disabilities. We are told in the Bampton Lectures (p. 144) " that our knowledge of God, though revealed by Himself, is revealed in relation to human faculties, and subject to the limitations and imperfections inseparable from the constitution of the human mind." Was it entirely beyond the power of the Creator so to form the minds of moral beings, that they should be capable of receiving, for the objects of their moral life, a real representation of Himself ? Was it not as easy in fact to do this, as to endow a preacher with the power of determining positively that it could not be done?

For "the pure in heart shall see God," we must substitute "shall see a regulative representation of God:" and that regulative representation will be equally seen by the pure and by the impure. We can no longer believe that depth and keenness of spiritual insight will increase with purity of life. The eye of a St. Paul can pierce no further into a symbol than the eye of any other man. Here, I venture to think, is a notable omission in Mr. Mansel's philosophy, and not in Mr. Mansel's philosophy alone.

The *hand* and the *eye* of God are not "regulative representations" but *figures;* as it is a *figure* when we speak of ourselves as seeing with our minds; and all "objections" to the use of the term *figure* in these cases are swallowed up in the fact that it alone expresses the truth. The *wisdom*, the *justice*, the *mercy*, the *love* of God are not figures, but realities, on which our moral life depends; and to confound them with things which are figures, by including all under the common name of "regulative representations," is a course which may have its advantages to a philosophical mind, but the advantages of which are swallowed up in the fact that it is fraught with most pernicious falsehood.

The world ought to view with jealousy the intro-
duction into religious matters of any strange terms.
For strange terms almost always cover falsehood,
which the use of plain language would at once
betray. The greatest things, when clearly and truly
apprehended, are capable of being as simply expressed as the least.

Mr. Mansel holds that the terms *hand*, *eye*,
power, *wisdom*, *goodness*, *anger*, *pity*, are "all, in
different degrees, condescensions to man's capacity
of thought." This being the case then, he has no
need of making any further superfœtations on a
language which already groans beneath the load.
He has only to say that the *goodness* of God is
a rather less bold figure than his *hand*.

It is evident that the notions which are carried to
so startling an extreme in the Bampton Lectures
originally arose in part from the idea that the moral
feelings were "perturbations," to use Bishop Copleston's term, and that therefore they were unworthy
of the Deity, and could be ascribed to him in Scripture only by "substitution" and "analogy," which
phrases are now received and issued anew as "regulative representation." But the truth is, the evil
feelings alone are "perturbations;" the good feelings, in a truly religious heart, are at once most
intense and most serene. They are the type and
the source of all serenity, and it is by virtue of their

presence that the beauty, grandeur, and repose of Nature produce in us the sensation of calm.

As to the knowledge which we ascribe to the Deity, it must be the same in kind with our knowledge; for we can no more represent to ourselves different kinds of knowledge or ignorance than we can represent to ourselves different kinds of morality. But the *modes* of acquiring knowledge, as well as the *extent* of knowledge, may be infinitely different; they differ greatly even among different men, and we do not feel in the slightest degree cut off from spiritual sympathy with our Maker by feeling assured, as we cannot help feeling assured, that the mode in which He knows all things, as well as the boundlessness of His knowledge, is utterly beyond our imagination.

In his Lectures, Mr. Mansel divided truths into Speculative and Regulative. But the class of speculative truths was left in the condition of a class without members; it appeared to be absolutely void.[1] And as " speculative truth " alone is what is called, in common language, *truth*, " regulative truth " being what is called, in common language, a *rule*, it seemed that mankind was left without anything that in plain and natural language would be called truth.[1] But an instance of " speculative truth " is now given. " It is a speculative truth to speak of

[1] See Mr. Chretien's ' Letter to the Rev. F. D. Maurice,' p. 18.

myself as seeing or hearing ; for the statement represents a fact of which I have direct knowledge from
my own experience." It appears then that facts
of experience are the only speculative truths, and
speculative truth being the highest, it is on the
lowest subjects only that the Creator has given us
the highest kind of truth.

I doubt, however, whether what Mr. Mansel says
in his Letter to me is consistent with what he had
said in his Bampton Lectures. In his Bampton
Lectures, (p. 143) adopting Kant's criticism
without reserve, he had actually swept away all
speculative truth whatever. And thus it was that
he was enabled to say that " it was strictly in
analogy with the method of God's Providence in
the constitution of man's mental faculties, to believe
that in Religion also He has given us truths
which are designed to be regulative rather than
speculative." But, if we are able by some of our
faculties to apprehend speculative truth, as Mr.
Mansel now admits that we are in the case of facts
of experience, the " analogy" of " Man's mental
constitution" fails. A contrary argument from
"analogy," if that term must be introduced, seems
to arise, indicating that as the Creator has given us
speculative truth in mere matters of sense, He will
not refuse it to us in matters on which our moral
being depends.

Still, all religious truth, even according to Mr.
Mansel's present position, is of the regulative, not of
the speculative kind. And yet here, I venture to
think, he is in a difficulty. For this truth, That all
religious truth is regulative, not speculative, must
itself be a speculative truth. So that Mr. Mansel
has destroyed all speculative truth in religion by
the exercise of a faculty which, according to his
theory, he does not possess. This is a trap-door
down which, if I mistake not, great sceptical
philosophers have fallen before.

"Action and not knowledge is man's destiny and
duty in this life."—Let us hope that these words
were not heard with too much complacency in the
national seat of knowledge, to whose members the
Bampton Lectures were delivered. I cannot help
thinking that we may learn a nobler sentiment—we
may learn that the pursuit of knowledge, above all
of spiritual knowledge, is one of the highest kinds
of action—from a teacher with whom the Lecturer
is well acquainted. On this subject, at least, Sir
William Hamilton can hardly be identified with his
disciple. "If the accomplishment of philosophy,"
he says, "imply a cessation of discussion,—if the
result of speculation be a paralysis of itself; the
consummation of knowledge is the condition of
intellectual barbarism. Plato has profoundly
defined man, 'the hunter of *truth*;' for in this

chase, as in others, the *pursuit* is all in all, the *success* comparatively nothing. ' Did the Almighty,' says Lessing, ' holding in his right hand *Truth*, and in his left *Search after Truth*, deign to proffer me the one I might prefer ; in all humility, but without hesitation, I should request—*Search after Truth.*' We *exist* only as we energize ; *pleasure* is the reflex of unimpeded energy ; energy is the mean by which our faculties are developed ; and a higher energy the *end* which their development proposes. In *action* is thus contained the existence, happiness, improvement, and perfection of our being ; and knowledge is only precious as it may afford a stimulus to the exercise of our powers, and the condition of our more complete activity." (On the Philosophy of Perception, p. 39.) Mr. Mansel's saying may possibly be a verbal echo of this passage, which, like that in his Lectures, declares knowledge to be subordinate to action. But if so, it is a strange echo, and strangely it would have sounded in Sir William Hamilton's ears.

It is merciful, however, to tell us that knowledge concerns us little, since we are to be told that " the truth of which our finite minds are susceptible may, for aught we know, be but the passing shadow of some higher reality, which exists only in the Infinite Intelligence." Assuredly a man will hardly give up the world and the things of sense, to follow that which for aught he knows, may be but a passing shadow.

Mr. Mansel gives us no explanation of the difficulty pointed out by me with regard to the position in which Theology, so far as it is concerned with the interpretation or with the rational application of Scripture, will be left when the Bible is reduced to a set of regulative representations. These regulative representations are addressed not to our moral sense and reason, but to our submission. They are not realities on which our minds can act, but modes in which an Omnipotent Ruler, of whom we know nothing, saving His manifestation of His power, wills that we shall think of Him. By what faculty can we interpret them? By what faculty can we deduce anything from them. What can the Theologian do with them but preserve them in safe custody like a sacred shield (if I may repeat my own illustration) which has fallen from Heaven, and which it is our duty to guard and adore, content with the evidence, or the tradition, of its having come down from the skies. There seems to be only this difference, that the Roman *ancile* fell at once and entire : whereas our *ancile* fell in a great number of pieces at different times, and we have no positive assurance that the whole has fallen yet. We may even now have only the fragment of a rule, which I venture to repeat is tantamount to no rule at all.

Again, by what faculty can we make deductions from regulative representations? You must let in reason and a rational conception of the Divine Nature if you wish to extend the import of one sentence beyond the range of its exact verbal signification, or to put two sentences together as premises, and draw from them a rational conclusion. I am very far from wishing to drive Mr. Mansel over a precipice in the matter of the Athanasian Creed, and assuredly I did not think that I was in the slightest degree impeaching his "orthodoxy" by showing that he had left himself no rational grounds for his belief. M. Charles Remusat, in the article to which I have alluded in my preface, specially mentions the Athanasian Creed as being a part of that theology which the Bampton Lectures have swept out of existence. I cannot help thinking that, rationally speaking, it is as M. Remusat says. I cannot help thinking that in the passage which I quoted in my "Postscript," Mr. Mansel destroyed every category of legitimate existence under which the Creed could possibly take shelter. The advocates of the formulary will scarcely find satisfaction in his present explanation. He quotes the words of some extreme Dogmatist — "Scriptura sacra theologiæ naturali adjumento est. Etenim in Scriptura sacra ea quoque de Deo docentur, quæ ex principiis rationis de eodem demonstrari possunt." And he then tells me that " whether a demonstration of this kind was the purpose of the Athanasian Creed, is a question on which he and I may differ, but that it is sufficient to say that he does not think such to have been its purpose. I confess that I fail to discern here any intelligible standing ground for the supporters of the Creed. The question is, not what were the " motives " of Mr. Mansel's reasonings, but what was their effect. It seems to me that their effect has been to render a great service to Christianity. I do not think that this formulary can long survive the blow he has given it. He, at all events, I am sure, will never again deem it consistent with his duty as a Christian to launch the sentence of everlasting condemnation against those who do not keep whole and undefiled a Creed about which he seems to admit there may be a natural difference of opinion, and the existence of which he is himself only able to defend in so very oblique and faltering a manner.

In this passage of his Letter, Mr. Mansel talks of " employing Reason in the interpretation of Scripture," as though it were a thing of which he approved. Let him only consider what this " Reason " is, what are its data, and whence it derives its authority. I am not without hopes that if he will go fairly into the question, he will end by giving up his general theory, and admitting the power of

Reason to attain speculative truth in religious matters and the existence of Rational Religion.

In his Lectures (p. 250) he speaks of God as
"making his own Revelation more perfect from
time to time." By which faculty does he discern
the more and the less perfect among "regulative
representations?" The power of discerning the
more and the less perfect implies a trustworthy
standard of comparison. Whence is Reason to obtain that standard? And if she possesses it, how
can Mr. Mansel put limits to her use of it? If she
is competent to pronounce that one part of a Revelation is less perfect, in other words, less Divine
than another part, why should she not be able to
say of an alleged Revelation that it is not Divine at
all? Is comparative lateness of date Mr. Mansel's
criterion of comparative perfection? Wherein consists the validity of such a criterion? In the case
of men, the latest addition to a work is, or is intended
to be, an improvement on the rest. But what
faculty has Mr. Mansel's theory left us, by which
we can undertake to say that the same is the case in
the works of God?

To distinguish between that which is essential
and that which is unessential, will be equally out
of our power. Any given part, however apparently
subordinate, of the set of regulative representations
which make up our divinely-imposed, but un-

intelligible, rule of thought and feeling, may be, so far at least as we can tell, quite as essential as those which are apparently the most important parts : just as the beads which make up a consecrated rosary, or the pieces of wood which a praying negro puts into his rotatory calabash, are all equally devoid of meaning, and equally full of supernatural virtue. And, this being the case, we fall into the perplexity which I have already pointed out to Mr. Mansel, and from which he does not attempt to relieve us, touching various readings and passages of disputed authenticity, on any one of which, for aught we can possibly know, the identity of the regulative representation, and with it our salvation, may depend. But, above all, we shall fall into desperate perplexity touching the Canon of Scripture, as to which there is so great a division among the Churches, though preachers may complacently assume that division is a thing unknown among the Churches, and found among the schools of philosophy alone.

Let Mr. Mansel, if he maintains his theory upon this subject, show us, how, upon the supposition that his theory is true, religion can subsist without an infallible Canon of Scripture ; and, if he finds that religion cannot subsist without an infallible Canon of Scripture, let him show how that infallible Canon can be obtained.

P

The writer in the Rambler who identified Mr. Mansel's scepticism with that of Dr. Newman, was certainly not far wrong ; but Dr. Newman, after rejecting Reason, has at least fairly embraced visible authority, and obtained whatever assurance it could afford. Mr. Mansel will, I apprehend, find that he has no refuge but historical and philological criticism, and that the comfort they, especially the first of them, will afford him in this matter of the Canon, will be very poor indeed.

Finally, the translation of "regulative representations" into another tongue than that in which they were given, seems a most precarious and even desperate operation. Their sanctity consists in their exact identity ; and who that knows anything of language, can feel confident that their exact identity will be preserved in the transition from one tongue to another. Every scholar is aware that our own admirable translation is in some passages not perfectly correct. Who can tell that these deviations from correctness are not fatal ; or that the spiritual life of our people, which the English Bible has sustained, has not been out of keeping with the authorized " representations," and therefore in fact no spiritual life at all ?

If I seem here to be pushing a theory to its extreme consequences, its author has done the same by the theories of his opponents. If he can fairly break the chain of my deductions by showing how, consistently with his philosophy, reason is competent to deal with Scripture, he may call my delineation of his philosophy a " caricature." But otherwise it must be accepted as a portrait, grotesque as it may seem.

To turn to the question of the Evidences. "The legitimate object of a rational criticism of revealed religion is not to be found in the *contents* of that religion, but in its *evidences*." (Bamp. Lect. p. 234) With this passage, which I quoted before, may be coupled another passage, " The conviction, *that* an Infinite Being exists, seems forced upon us by the manifest incompleteness of our finite knowledge; but we have no rational means whatever of determining *what* is the nature of that Being. The mind is thus perfectly blank with regard to any speculative representation of the Divine Essence; and for that very reason, Philosophy is not entitled, on internal evidence, to accept any, or to reject any. The only question which we are reasonably at liberty to ask in this matter, relates to the Evidences of the Revelation as a fact. If there is sufficient evidence, on other grounds, to shew that the Scripture, in which this doctrine is contained, is a Revelation from God, the doctrine itself must be unconditionally received, not as reasonable, nor as unreasonable, but as scriptural.

If there is not such evidence, the doctrine itself
will lack its proper support ; but the Reason
which rejects it is utterly incompetent to substitute any other representation in its place."
(p. 180) No one, it appears to me, can read
these two passages attentively without seeing that
they deny all those moral evidences of the Christian Revelation which reason draws from the character of its contents, and place it absolutely on
a level with the foulest and most demoralizing
superstition on earth which can allege miracles
in its favour. Miracles are the sole remaining
proofs of a Religion. It must be owned that
their efficacy, as proofs, in Mr. Mansel's eyes, is
great indeed. "If a single miracle," he says,
"is once admitted as supported by competent
evidence, the entire history is at once removed
from the ordinary calculations of more or less
probability. One miracle is sufficient to shew
that the series of events, with which it is connected, is one which the Almighty has seen fit
to mark by exceptions to the ordinary course
of His Providence : and this being once granted,
we have no *a priori* grounds to warrant us in
asserting that the number of such exceptions
ought to be larger or smaller." (p. 252.) The
Egyptian sorcerers performed not only one miracle,
but three. What was the effect of those three mira-

cles on the mythical history of Egypt, and the
national worship of animals and plants ? Was it to
put them above the criticism of human reason ?

Mr. Mansel says that the first of the two passages above quoted is followed by a sentence "in
which it is expressly maintained" (I think it
would have been rather more accurate to say admitted) " that the contents of a Revelation are
included among its Evidences." We have, then,
these three propositions :—the evidences of a religion are the legitimate object of rational criticism;
the contents of a religion are not the legitimate
object of a rational criticism ; the contents are a
part of the evidences. Whence it seems to follow
that a part of the evidences, viz. :—the contents,
both are and are not the legitimate object of a
rational criticism.

Even this admission however is soon virtually with-
drawn ; and it appears that the difference between
recognizing the contents of a religion as evidences,
and refusing to recognize them, is the difference
between nothing and negation. For Mr. Mansel
comes round (p. 238) to the conclusion that " The
evidence derived from the internal character of a
religion, whatever may be its value within its
proper limits, *is, as regards the divine origin of the
religion, purely negative.* It may prove in certain
cases (though even here the argument requires much

caution in its employment) that a religion *has not*
come from God ; but it is in no case sufficient to
prove that it has come from Him." Mr. Mansel's
opponents may safely challenge him to reconcile
the admission of the moral evidences, even as negative proofs, with his general theory as to our total
ignorance of God. If we have " no rational means
whatever of determining what is the nature of the
Infinite Being," we can have no rational means of
determining, by reference to His nature, what does
not come from Him any more than what *does*. But
we may waive that question. It is quite startling
enough to have been led by a defender of Christianity to the conclusion that the teaching of its
Founder has only a negative advantage, as regards
the proof which its character affords of its divine
origin, over the teaching of Mahomet.

That we should found religion on miracles alone
is, I apprehend, clearly a necessary result of Mr.
Mansel's general philosophy. If our moral nature
is not identical with that of our Maker, and we have
not that organ of sympathy and intercourse with
Him, no channel is left through which He can
manifest Himself to us, if He wishes to do so, but
that of our senses, which He may strike by visible
miracles. And yet the task still remains before
Mr. Mansel of constructing a philosophy of miracles,
and showing how, all other grounds being removed,

they can form the basis of a religion. An unusual phenomenon occurs in the physical world. I simply see the occurrence, knowing absolutely nothing, according to the present hypothesis, of the power from which it comes : and thereupon I am called upon to adopt a new religion. It seems to me that this is a desperate leap in the dark.

I pointed out to Mr. Mansel that we could not, without constructing the forbidden Philosophy of the Absolute, regard the miracles as exhibitions of Divine love, because, in so doing, we should assume that human love was Divine, and that we must consequently regard them only as exhibitions of power. He rejoins that the conception of *power* is human as well as that of *love*. I am inclined to think it is so ; and thus the last support is cut away. There remains to us no evidence, either external or internal, to prove that religion comes from God.

Turn whichever way we will, it appears that when God has given man reason, it is perilous for divines to attempt to take it away.

Mr. Mansel has appealed in his Letter to a summary of Christian Evidences in one of the rhetorical passages of his book, as showing that he includes the moral evidences among the rest. I have admitted in the most distinct and emphatic terms, and I again most distinctly and emphatically admit the happy inconsistency which appears between his phi-

losophy and the personal convictions displayed
in his rhetorical passages. I can only add the expression of my unfeigned surprise that, with his great
acuteness, he should fail to see that the eloquent
summary of moral Evidences to which he appeals,
blows the philosophy of his book to the four winds.

If we believe in a Maker of the Universe, it
is mere madness to doubt that He can, if He
pleases, suspend the operation of the laws which
He has Himself made. There is no need to introduce so strange an apparatus as the theory of
a higher law of nature intersecting and super-
seding the ordinary laws from time to time. In a
world ruled by Divine Goodness, a miracle is natural, if it can serve any good end. The word *law*,
as denoting the regular course of the material world,
though, strictly speaking, improper and fallacious,
has become too well established to be discarded.
But it must always be remembered that what is a
law to Nature, and, in a certain sense, as regulating
the course of our life, a law to us, is to the Creator
merely a mode of action, absolutely variable at His
pleasure. Only of this we may be assured, that if
the Creator performs a miracle, He will perform it,
as He does everything else, for a moral end. He
will not do it from caprice, like earthly despotism
displaying its petty power; nor will He do it to
encourage the vice of superstition.

There may well have been a moral end for the performance of miracles, at the time when Christianity was to be introduced into the world. At the present time, seeing Christianity, as we do, in its place in history; comparing it, as we now can, with everything else that history discloses; observing its effects in the regeneration of the world; and estimating, by the aid of that which is decried as 'philosophy,' the type of character displayed in the Life of its Founder; we have overwhelming grounds, of a strictly rational kind, for pronouncing it to be Divine. But they to whom it first presented itself had no such grounds. And if it was desirable, in the interest of mankind, that they should receive it as superhuman, and preserve and propagate it accordingly at the sacrifice of all their earthly pleasures, and at the risk of their lives, it cannot be thought unreasonable that they should have, in addition to the moral character by which it commanded and won their hearts, such evidence of its superhuman origin as their simple minds were able to apprehend. To have advanced their minds eighteen centuries, would have been to put them out of harmony with the generation amidst which and on which they were to act; and unless their minds had been advanced eighteen centuries, it is difficult to imagine how, without miracles, they would have

Q

certainly known that which it was essential they should certainly know.

The occurrence of miracles, then, at the time when the Gospel was first published, presents nothing from which reason need in the least degree recoil. But that a man should desire, and be content, to ground Religion exclusively on the evidence of miracles, and think that in doing so he is paying a special tribute of reverence to God, appears strange indeed.

In the first place, what can be more irrational or more derogatory to the Deity, than to deny or disregard His presence in the order, beauty, and excellence which appear in the regular government of His universe, and to acknowledge it only in occasional interruptions?

In the second place, those who imagine that in founding religion on miracles, they are renouncing and degrading human reason, which alone of all the works of the Creator they take to be evil, are exceedingly mistaken. They are in fact founding religion not only upon human reason, but upon its very frailest and most precarious product, historical evidence. They constantly assume that they have themselves seen the miracles, or at least that they have some assurance of their reality equivalent to the assurance which sense gives us of outward things, and which consciousness gives us of things existing and passing in the mind. This assumption is facilitated and indeed rendered almost inevitable in the case of ordinary minds by the lessons of childhood, which impress the miracles on our minds and almost on our sense as unquestionable facts, without any examination or even mention of the evidence, and before the critical faculty has had time to awake. But the truth of course is, that the only thing of which we are immediately and certainly cognizant, is a record containing the evidence of human witnesses, the authenticity and trustworthiness of which require to be established by a critical process, not only of a rational, but of a very intricate kind.

Mr. Mansel even seems disposed to hold that the examination of the Evidences (which, as I think I have shown, must, on his theory, be reduced to the Historical Evidences) forms in itself "an ample field for the use of reason," without opening any of the subjects of inquiry on which his philosophy has put a seal. This seems to imply, that the subject of the Evidences is one which presents abundant matter for discussion, involving, of course, the possibility of discrepancy in the conclusions.

If it is into the Court of Historical Criticism that we are ultimately to go, we shall find it a strict court, with rigorous rules, the stringency of which is not diminished but increased when the fact in question is of vital importance. "It seems to be often believed," says a great master of historical investigation, "and, at all events, it is perpetually assumed in practice, that historical evidence is different in its nature from other sorts of evidence. Until this error is effectually extirpated, all historical researches must lead to uncertain results. Historical evidence, like judicial evidence, is founded on the testimony of credible witnesses. Unless these witnesses had personal and immediate perception of the facts which they report, unless they saw and heard what they relate as having happened, their evidence is not entitled to credit."[1] To which it must be added that in order to know that a witness had personal and immediate perception of the facts which he reports, we must have his positive statement, directly or by clear implication, to that effect.

I apprehend that if we proceed in this inquiry by the strict rules of historical criticism, a good deal will be found to turn upon the degree of certainty with which we can identify the authors of the Gospels with persons stated in them to have had "personal and immediate perception" of the miracles. In other words, a good deal will turn upon the authorship of the First and Fourth Gospels. Mr. Mansel's distinguished successor in the Bampton Lectureship, after an examination of the evidence,

[1] Sir G. C. Lewis on the Credibility of Early Roman History, p. 15.

appears to entertain no doubt upon this point. " In truth," he says, " there is not the slightest pretence for insinuating that there was ever any doubt as to the authorship of any one of the historical books of the New Testament, which are as uniformly ascribed to the writers whose names they bear, as the Return of the Ten Thousand to Xenophon, or the Lives of the Cæsars to Suetonius. There is, indeed, *far better* evidence of authorship in the case of the four Gospels and of the Acts of the Apostles, than exists with respect to the works of almost any classical writer. It is a very rare occurrence for classical works to be distinctly quoted, or for their authors to be mentioned by name, within a century of the time of their publication." [1] He cites, as instances of this fact respecting the classics, Herodotus, Thucydides, Polybius, Livy, and Tacitus. In the first two cases the name of the author is actually embodied in the text. In no one of the five cases could there be the slightest motive for attributing the work to the person whose name it bears, if it was not known to be his; whereas there was obviously the strongest motive for attributing a Gospel of uncertain authorship to an Apostle. But the defect of testimony to the authorship of the classics would not cure the defect of testimony to the authorship of the Gospels, and I confess I should shudder if I were told that

[1] Rawlinson's Bampton Lectures, p. 199.

the fate of religion and of the world turned upon the authenticity even of the most undoubtedly authentic among the classics.

Sir G. C. Lewis's proposition that historical evidence does not differ from other evidence requires one important qualification. Historical evidence differs most disadvantageously from other evidence in this respect, that the witnesses are dead and in case of dispute cannot be interrogated : so that a doubt once fairly raised must remain a doubt for ever. It must remain a doubt for ever, and the alleged fact to which it attaches, though it may be spoken of as probable, if the balance of evidence inclines to the affirmative side, can never, if we respect the rule of veracity, be spoken of as certain.

The rules of this inquiry we must take not from the desires of our hearts but from the Science of Evidence. And as to the spirit in which we are to enter on the inquiry, few would deny in terms that it ought to be that of absolute reliance on the Author of Truth. If He has not given us conclusive evidence of any fact which we may imagine to be of vital importance to us, it must be because that fact is not of vital importance to us in His eyes, and because He does not desire that it should be an essential part of our faith. It may be, that with a view to the purposes for

which He made the Moral World, He desires that
the religion of moral beings should rest on evidence of a moral kind, not on the evidence of
physical signs and wonders. But whatever may
be His purpose, and the course of His Providence
in the matter, of this we are certain, that He
will accept only the homage of truth, not 'the
unclean sacrifice of a lie.' The 'faith' with which
we are often called upon to eke out the defect of
historical evidences when the artifices of apologists
can stretch them no further, is, if we will fairly
look into it, nothing more or less than a practice
of saying that proof is complete when we know
that it is incomplete, by way of performing an act
of piety towards God. If we cast our consciences
under the Car of Falsehood in this manner, we
must leave the worship of Juggernaut alone.

'Minute cavils' is the name applied by Mr.
Mansel to objections which, I firmly believe may
be conclusively answered, but which have deeply
moved the heart of Europe, and turned away
thousands of educated men from Christ. It is
to be hoped that the clergy will not go forth into
the world in its present state, thinking that they
have only minute cavils to encounter.

There is, indeed, independently of the mere historical evidence, evidence of a moral kind which
may be adduced, and with great force, in sup-

port of the Gospel miracles. They bear the seal of a spiritual purpose widely distinguishing them from the mere exhibitions of power which man, in a primitive age, if left to himself, imagines as the manifestations of divinity. They are not only or principally acts of power, but of Divine Beneficence. They form an entirely harmonious part of a character which, as I have elsewhere[1] endeavoured to show, a sound historical criticism must pronounce to be entirely out of the natural course of history, and therefore superhuman. This evidence stands on the same ground as the other moral evidences : that is to say, on the surest ground on which evidence can possibly stand.

I confess that I, for one, enter with the less anxiety into any question concerning the validity of mere historical evidence, because I am convinced that no question concerning the validity of mere historical evidence can be absolutely vital to religion. Historical evidence is not a ground upon which religion can possibly rest : for the human testimony of which such evidence consists is always fallible ; the chance of error can never be excluded : and the extraordinary delusions into which great bodies of men have fallen show that even in the case of a multitude of witnesses that chance may be present

[1] In a Lecture on " Some supposed consequences of the decline of historical progress."

in a considerable degree, particularly if the scene of
the alleged fact is laid in an uncritical age or
nation.[1] Probable evidence, therefore, is the highest
we can have of any historical fact. In ordinary
cases we practically need no higher. The great
results of history are here : we have and enjoy them
as certainly as we have and enjoy any object of
sense ; and it signifies little by what exact agency
in any particular case the work of human progress
was carried on. But in the case of a religion
probable evidence will not suffice. Religion is not
a speculation which we may be content to hold
subject to a certain chance of error, nor is it a
practical interest of the kind which Butler has in
his mind when he tells us that we must act on this,
as in other cases, on probability. It is a spiritual
affection which nothing less than the assured
presence of its object can excite. We may be
quite content to hold that the Life of Cæsar was
such as it is commonly taken to have been, subject
to certain chances of error arising from his own
bias as an autobiographer, and from the partiality,
prejudice, or imperfect information of his con-
temporaries ; but we should not be content to hold

---

[1] I say 'age or nation.' We frequently hear divines repeating that
the Gospel miracles took place in the age of Tacitus. They took place
in the age, but not in the country of Tacitus. The present is a critical
age in England and Germany, but not in Turkey or Spain.

R

any vital fact of our religion under the same
conditions. We may be ready to stake, and do
constantly stake, our worldly interests, as Butler
truly observes, upon probabilities, when certainty is
beyond our power. But our hearts would refuse
their office, if we were to bid them adore and hold
communion with a probable God.

The historical evidences of religion are necessarily
and inherently of less than adamantine strength.
The moral evidences are adamantine. And as was
before intimated, there seems to be nothing contrary
to reason in the supposition that the religion of
Man, as a Moral Being, may have been intended
by his Maker to rest upon moral, not upon physical
grounds.

Yet a certain school of religious philosophers
appear to cling to the last remnant of the arbitrary
and the marvellous in nature, as though it were the
last strong-hold of religion. Mr. Mansel himself
seems to regard with great religious complacency
the fact that the variableness of the weather still
baffles science ; and he is inclined to ground on
this fact, among others, a peculiar theory as to the
ways of Providence in its dealings with Man. But
in the first place, the weather, though variable in
England, is comparatively stable on the continent,
and still more stable between the tropics ; and it
cannot be supposed that the ways of Providence, in

dealing with man, are affected by the latitude and longitude. In the second place, it must surely strike us as strange to see Providence thus driven up, as it were, into a corner by the progress of scientific inquiry, and the Creator on the point of being ejected from His own world by the operation of a love of inquiry which He has Himself implanted, and of faculties for inquiry which He has Himself bestowed. Suppose the meteorological observations, which are now going on, should result in the reduction of the weather to general laws. Let us trust that, in that case, nobody will be led to refer to the Bampton Lectures for 1858 : for if any one does, he will find that the councils of Providence have come into collision with human science ; and that, after a protracted struggle, human science has at length gained the day.

It appeared to me and to others that, by the reasonings of the Bampton Lectures, not only Morality and Truth, but the Deity Himself, as an object of our belief, was swept away. On this last point Mr. Mansel's present Letter gives us even less satisfaction than on the other two.

He stakes the existence of a God, as far as Man is concerned, on the possibility of our believing in that "which we are unable to fix in any human conception." And it is necessary for the object of his theory that he should do so. For if man is able to form a conception of God, however imperfect, there will be, to the extent of that conception, and of the legitimate inferences from it, a Rational Theology; while if man is unable to believe in a God, there can be, as Mr. Mansel himself says, ' no Theology' at all.

To prove that it is possible to believe in the existence of that " which cannot be fixed in any human conception," an appeal is made to passages from the works of several divines ; among others, to the rhetorical passages of Hooker and St. Augustine which I have before mentioned, to a passionate sentence of Jacobi, and to the quotation from Beveridge, also before mentioned, in which *conceive* is used as a synonym for *understand.* As to Beveridge, he in the very same passage explains how we can have *the clearest apprehension* of the Deity ; and while he says that he *cannot conceive* how God is of Himself infinitely holy, just, and powerful, he says that he *can conceive* how He is without body, parts, and passions.

To go through the works of these Divines, in order to settle the exact meaning attached by each to phrases which were evidently not used with a knowledge of the present issue, would be a very long and not a very satisfactory process. There is, if I mistake not, a shorter road to our mark. The propositions that God *exists*, and that He is our

Sustainer and *Governor*, are laid down by Mr. Mansel (Lect. p. 170), as the three which form "the great foundation of all religious belief whatever," and on the possibility of believing in which, though inconceivable, depends "the possibility of any Revelation at all." Now these three propositions, logically speaking, are *judgments*. And a *judgment* is defined in Mr. Mansel's *Prolegomena Logica* (p. 60) as "a combination of two *concepts*, related to one or more common objects of possible intuition." The subjects, then, of the three propositions affirming severally that God exists, and that He is our Sustainer and Governor, must be *concepts*. Does Mr. Mansel require us to fix in a *concept* that "which we cannot fix in any human *conception*?"

The Lecturer evidently regards Revelation as a series of propositions in Theology, miraculously made known by God to Man. What is the subject of those propositions? Is it a word that has any meaning, or a word that has none? If it is a word that has meaning, what can that meaning be but a human conception, the product of human thought? If it is a word that has no meaning, how much meaning will there be in the Revelation which the propositions compose?

To put the same thing in another way : Mr. Mansel has reduced Deity, antecedently to Revelation, to a " Negative Idea." How can the Revelation of a negative idea be anything but a negative Revelation?

I reminded Mr. Mansel before that Revelation was the voice of God: and I asked him how we could know the voice, if the speaker was unknown? To this question he makes no reply.

The task, however, which he has imposed upon the human mind is, in fact, still harder than that of believing in a thing which we are unable to fix in any human conception. In requiring us to affirm with him that "there is an Absolute Morality based upon, or rather identical with, the Eternal Nature of God," he requires us not only to believe, by separate acts of the mind, in two things, each of which we are unable to fix in any human conception, but also to believe that one of these two things is *identical with*, or rather *based upon*, the other. Those who wish to measure the difficulty of this mental operation must have due regard to the separate relations denoted by *based upon* and *identical* respectively, and to the shade of difference which the balancing of the writer's mind between the two, and his inclination in favour of identity, imply as existing between them.

In his Bampton Lectures, (p. 107) Mr. Mansel, while tearing away, as he imagined, the supports of Rational Religion, wrote as follows, "Conscious-"ness, in its earliest discernible form, is only pos-

" sible as the result of an union of the reflective
" with the intuitive faculties. A state of mind, to
" be known at all as existing, must be distinguished
" from other states ; and to make this distinction we
" must think of it as well as experience it. Without
" thought as well as sensation, there could be no
" consciousness of the existence of an external world :
" without thought as well as emotion and volition
" there could be no consciousness of the moral na-
" ture of man. Sensation without thought would
" at most amount to no more than an indefinite
" sense of uneasiness or momentary irritation, with-
" out any power of discerning in what manner we
" are affected, or of distinguishing our successive
" affections from each other. To distinguish, for
" example, in the visible world, any one object from
" any other, to know the house as a house, or the
" tree as a tree, we must be able to refer them
" to distinct notions ; and such reference is an act
" of thought. The same condition holds good of
" the religious consciousness also. In whatever
" mental affection we become conscious of our
" relation to a Supreme Being, we can discern
" that consciousness, as such, only by reflecting
" upon it as conceived under its proper notion.
" Without this, we could not know our religious
" consciousness to be what it is : and, as the
" knowledge of a fact of consciousness is identical

" with its existence,—without this, the religious
" consciousness as such, could not exist." This
passage appeared to me in effect to prove a belief
in God to be impossible to the human mind. The
reasoning seemed to be in substance this—' We can
have no distinct knowledge of anything, unless we
can refer it to a class of objects, and thus distinguish it in our minds from objects of a different
class ; and that of which we have no distinct knowledge has to our minds no existence. Now there
is no class of objects to which we can properly refer
God ; therefore we can have no distinct knowledge
of God ; therefore to our minds God has no existence ?' I did not for a moment imagine that
Mr. Mansel meant to prove belief in God to be
impossible, but it appeared to me that he had
inadvertently done so. It appeared to me that he
had intended, by a decisive stroke of his metaphysical weapon, to destroy once for all the testimony of reason ; and that the testimony of our
reason, being the only testimony which Providence
has afforded us, he had, in fact, destroyed more
than he intended. And this, I venture to think,
is the general moral of his book.

He now tells me that " the only apparent force
in my reasoning is due to a confusion between
the *conception* of the Relative and the *belief* in
the Absolute."

I conceive God under certain relations, every one of which is a "notion" analogous to the notions which we form of other objects. The terms, Father, Ruler, Judge, Good, Wise, Just, all represent notions derived in the first instance from human relations, and applied to God, not as exactly expressing the perfection of His absolute nature, but as expressing the nearest approach to it which we are capable of receiving. In other words: I *conceive* God under certain notions derived from the things of this world : I *believe* that these notions only faintly and partially express the infinite perfections of His absolute nature, which I do not conceive. And therefore it is, that, believing as I do, and as you do not, that there may be regulative truths founded on analogy, where there cannot be speculative truths founded on identity or exact resemblance, I am able to assent entirely to the language of Bishop Browne on this subject : " Insomuch that our conceptions and expressions of these perfections, though in their first and strictly proper acceptation they be merely human, are all yet apt and necessary when spoken of God; and there is nothing the less of truth and reality in this analogy, because we are not able to discern any exact degree and proportion, or that particular sort of similitude which is the ground and foundation of it. Though we do not appre-hend it now, yet there is a reason in the very nature of things divine why they should be conceived and expressed after that manner they now are, rather than after any other ; insomuch that we then think justly, and express our thoughts of them in the greatest aptness and propriety of speech our present condition of infirmity will admit."—(Letter, p. 36).

I, of course, accept without hesitation an author's version of his own meaning ; though I accept it, I must confess, as the author himself accepts the ' Absolute,' without attaching to it any very definite mode of thought. If I were to attempt to comment on it, I should say that it appears some-what to alter the drift of the original passage, which, at all events, was destructive, whereas the present gloss upon it is constructive ; the gloss showing us how we *can*, whereas the original passage showed us how we *could not* apprehend God. But I will

s

not attempt to comment. I will only beg leave to say that my error was excusable, and that other readers of the Lectures may be excused if, in the absence of this commentary, they fall into the same error ; since neither in the passage itself, nor in its immediate context, is there any mention of the ' Relative' or the 'Absolute,' nor any words insisting on the distinction between a belief in the existence of a thing and a conception. The subject of the passage is the 'religious consciousness,' and I venture to say, the mass of readers will construe it as proving, not that we can conceive the Relative while we can only believe in the Absolute, but that, to us, the religious consciousness or, to speak plainly, the Deity does not exist.

" Religion, to be a relation between God and Man at all, must rest on *a belief in the Infinite* and also on a belief in the Finite ; for, if we deny the first, there is no God, and if we deny the second, there is no Man." (Lect. p. 182). Let us combine with this another proposition—(p. 72)—" If all thought is limitation ;—if whatever we conceive is by the very act of conception regarded as finite,—the *infinite*, from a human point of view, *is merely a name for the absence of those conditions under which thought is possible.*" According to these two propositions, taken together, it would appear that all religion rests on a belief in the absence, in a

particular case, of those conditions under which
thought is possible ; in other words, on belief in an
intellectual void.

Mr. Mansel must observe that the inability of
the human mind to form a conception of the Deity,
which he imagines himself to have demonstrated,
would not be cured by any Revelation. For that
inability is a defect inherent in the structure of the
mind itself, not a lack of clearness in the object to
which the mind is directed. It is a want of the
power of sight, not a dimness or remoteness of the
thing to be seen. In vain will the light of Revelation be unveiled, if it is to stream only on the
sightless eyeballs of the blind. Again I say,
this is the Nemesis of Orthodoxy borrowing
weapons from Rationalism to destroy Rational
Religion.

In the same way, all the metaphysical difficulties
which Mr. Mansel raises through so many pages,
by playing off, in a variety of ingenious forms, the
antagonism between the Infinite and the Finite, if
they are formidable to any religion, are formidable alike to all. At the foundation of every
religion, if of any, we shall meet with the " self-
contradictions" which this antagonism produces ;
and in no case can Man be made really to believe
in the self-contradictory, though he may, by means
of certain appliances, be made to say that he believes

in it, by way of paying a pious tribute of hypocrisy to God.

The fact, however, is, that these difficulties are not very formidable to any religion. Mr. Mansel, as I have pointed out, and he does not deny, has inadvertently turned *Infinite*, which is the mere negative of *Finite*, and can have no positive meaning, except as a rhetorical synonym for *vast*, into a positive term. A mere negative cannot possibly come into collision or antagonism of any kind with any positive thing or idea whatever. But Mr. Mansel, in the passages to which I refer, evidently conceives of the *Infinite* as an immeasurable mass, thrusting the Finite out of existence. By thinking of this, an uncomfortable sensation is, no doubt, produced in the mind ; just as, by thinking of an interminable train of moving objects, a sleepy sensation is produced : and I believe it would be as rational to be influenced by one sensation as by the other in the choice of a religion. Yet to these reasonings, delivered by a great divine, a learned University listened hour after hour, and, no doubt, saw Rational Religion put beneath its feet.

When imposing terms, such as " The Infinite," " The Finite," " The Absolute," " The Relative," " The Unconditional," " Regulative and Speculative Truth," " Regulative Representations," are uttered over the heads of an audience by a preacher of undoubted orthodoxy and most eminent learning, the hearers, as the reasoning passes their comprehension, naturally conclude that it is irrefragable, and that all persons, except those who think as they do, have been left without a God.

In one place (p. 25), Mr. Mansel dilates on "the melancholy spectacle of the household of humanity divided against itself, the reason against the feelings, and the feelings against the reason, and the dim half-consciousness of the shadow of the Infinite frowning down upon both." If I am not mistaken, we might as well allow the frown of a negative particle, as the frown of the " Infinite," to cast its shadow over our souls.

We are told (p. 54) that the " web of contra-dictions," which is woven out of the " impossibility of conceiving the co-existence of the Infinite and Finite, and the cognate impossibility of conceiving a first commencement of phenomena, or the Absolute giving truth to the Relative," might be " prolonged to a still greater length" than the Bampton Lecturer has prolonged it. I have no doubt it might be prolonged not only to a greater, but to an indefinite length, if, being exempted at once from the restraints of common sense and the limit of mortality, we were set at liberty to talk to eternity without mean-ing. But as the metaphysic shuttle, when it seemed to weave the woof, would, in fact, be flying to and fro full of nothing, the web of contradiction would scarcely be strong enough to restrain the struggles of a very powerful mind.

A philosopher who should resolve ‘ the existence of Moral Evil in the world ’ into ‘ an aspect of the mystery respecting the co-existence of the Finite and the Infinite,’ would, I believe, perform incomparably the greatest service ever rendered to mankind.

The case of the *Relative* and the *Absolute*, seems to be precisely parallel to that of the *Finite* and *Infinite*. *Absolute* is merely the negative of *Relative*, as *Infinite* is of *Finite*. It is a mere synonym for *Unrelated*. If therefore any man has made himself uneasy by attempting to conceive of the ‘Absolute’ as a positive being, and to imagine it “ giving birth to the Relative,” the best advice to offer him is apparently that offered by Abernethy to a patient, who told him that when he held his arm out in a particular way it gave him pain, and was rather bluntly recommended not to hold out his arm in that way.

Nor is there any property or power in the adjectives *Infinite* and *Absolute* which there is not in the factitious substantives *the Infinite* and *the Absolute*. It is expected that our reason will be stricken with impotence by the questions ‘ How can Infinite Power be able to do all things, and yet Infinite Goodness be unable to do evil? How can Infinite Justice exact the utmost penalty for every sin, and yet Infinite Mercy pardon the sinner? How can Infinite Wisdom know all that is to come, and yet Infinite Freedom be at liberty to do or forbear?' The reply of reason is, that the compatibility of power to do evil with forbearance to do it, the compatibility of justice with mercy, the compatibility of foreknowledge of our own actions, resulting from a settled character, with perfect freedom of action, are things more or less enigmatic; but that they are not made at all more enigmatic by introducing the word *Infinite*. A character which should be such as at once to "exact the utmost penalty for every sin" and yet "show pardon to the sinner," in other words, a character which should be at once merciful and merciless, would no doubt present a moral enigma of no ordinary kind. But in compounding this character Mr. Mansel uses "Infinite Justice" as "No Mercy," and "Infinite Mercy' as "No Justice."

In another passage, (p. 175), the Lecturer endeavours to overwhelm us by analyzing the Divine Essence and exhibiting a plurality of Attributes, each infinite in its kind, and yet all together constituting but one Infinite. "That there can be but one Infinite," he says "appears to be a

necessary conclusion of reasoning ; for diversity
is itself a limitation : yet here we have many
Infinites, each distinct from the other, yet all
constituting one Infinite, which is neither identical with them, nor distinguishable from them."
Here again, the negative term *Infinite*, as it adds
nothing to the idea, adds nothing to the difficulty,
which is simply that of conceiving a number of
different attributes making up one character ; and
is to be surmounted, perhaps, mainly by ceasing
to use improper and exaggerated language about
the "distinctness" and the "mutual limitation"
of attributes which even in human character, as
it approaches perfection, are always tending to
fusion, and which therefore in the Nature to which
human virtue remotely points, we may divine to
be simply one.

In one passage of the Bampton Lectures, (p. 89)
we are told that " it is our duty to think of God as
personal, and it is our duty to believe that he is
Infinite." In another place, (p. 85) we are told
that "to speak of an Absolute and Infinite Person
is simply to use language to which, however true
it may be in a superhuman sense, no mode of
human thought can possibly attach itself." The
duty of "*thinking*" of the Deity as that to which
"*no mode of human thought* can possibly attach
itself" will, it is to be feared, prove very arduous

to the human mind. But perhaps it may be lightened by recollecting that the difficulty, such as it is, attaches not to the epithets ' Absolute ' and ' Infinite,' which have here no meaning whatever, but to *personality*, which, whether it be Divine or human, is an abstraction, and, like other abstractions, incapable of being represented by the imagination, though it is intelligible to the understanding.

I wish I could breathe into the earth which received the fatal secret of Midas's ears, what I am now going to say. This discussion has had the effect of strongly confirming and increasing an irreverent suspicion, which I had long entertained, that the "Absolute" and the "Unconditional" are mere arbitrary notions, bearing no sort of relation to any realities whatever ; and that the controversy about them, though it is generally assumed to be one of the highest interest to the community, is a mere clashing together of metaphysical cymbals, without any meaning, and without a possibility of any tangible result. To me it seems that Mr. Mansel is triumphant, and that he drags the Germans captive behind his car, so long as he is arguing, in effect, that the Absolute and the Unconditional are nonentities, and that nothing but nonsense can be founded on them. But when he admits, as he constantly does, that these entities exist and are of the highest importance, and

T

yet denies that it is possible for the human mind to apprehend them, I cannot help thinking that he must have unconsciously performed the feat the possibility of which he denies.

At all events, it is satisfactory to receive from one who is perfectly master of the subject, definitions of the Absolute and the Infinite, as well as of the metaphysical First Cause (the source of similar perplexities), which prove that these entities are not identical with the Deity as He is actually manifested to us, and consequently that no difficulties or contradictions connected with them can embarrass our practical religion. " To conceive the Deity as He is," says Mr. Mansel (Bampton Lect. p. 45), " we must conceive Him as First Cause, as Absolute, and as Infinite. By the *First Cause* is meant that which produces all things, and is itself produced of none. By the *Absolute*, is meant that which exists in and by itself, having no necessary relation to any other being. By the *Infinite* is meant that which is free from all possible limitation ; that than which a greater is inconceivable, and which consequently can receive no additional attribute or mode of existence which it had not from all eternity." Now, the Deity is not, in this sense, the *First Cause*, since He does not produce the free actions of men in the same sense in which He produces the objects and events of the material world. He is not the *Abso-*

lute, since He has a necessary relation to every object of His Providence and Affection. He is not the *Infinite,* since He is limited by the free personality which He has bestowed on Man, and he does receive additional attributes and modes of existence as often as He becomes the Father of new beings and the object of new worship.

The difficulty which is conjured up out of the antagonism between *liberty* and *necessity* is like the rest of these metaphysical difficulties, equally fatal to all religions, if it is fatal to any. But this difficulty is very simply solved by pointing out that the term *liberty* requires qualification, and that the term *necessity* is untrue.

There is another religious difficulty about *time.* " Every object, of whose existence we can be in any way conscious, is necessarily apprehended by us as succeeding in *time* to some former object of consciousness, and as itself occupying a certain portion of time " (p. 78). This, too, if it affects religion at all, leads to universal atheism. But the reason of mankind, ever presumptuous, has in this, as in many other instances, dealt rather rudely with metaphysical ' necessities.' It corrects, by an effort of reflection, what it knows to be a mere defect of the imagination, or presentative faculty, and worships an Eternal Deity.

. There is another difficulty as to the connection

between Mind and Matter. We do not know how
our sensations and volitions pass from the body to
the mind, and from the mind to the body. Nor do
we know the exact functions of the spleen. But
how does either of those circumstances affect
rational religion?

Again, there is the religious difficulty of "the
Infinite divisibility of extension:" in other words,
the puzzle of Achilles and the tortoise. This, too,
leads, if to anything, to universal atheism. When
we have added to it the difficulty of squaring the
circle, and that of discovering perpetual motion, the
list of our religious difficulties will, we may hope,
be complete.

"If I build again the things which I have
destroyed, I make myself a transgressor,"—such is
the Scriptural denunciation, which, by a somewhat
liberal construction, Mr. Mansel applies to certain
German philosophers, who, having destroyed the
foundations of religion in the speculative intellect,
have attempted to give it new foundations in our
Moral Nature. In his own Lectures, having, so far
as the speculative reason is concerned, destroyed the
religious consciousness, he proceeds (p. 108) to
build it up again out of certain "individual states
of mind, in which is presented, as an immediate
fact, that relation of Man to God, of which Man,
by reflection, may become distinctly and definitely

conscious." Thus he hopes to obtain a basis for religion, without admitting the exercise of the speculative reason.

"Two such states," he says "may be specified, as dividing between them the rude materials out of which Reflection builds up the edifice of Religious Consciousness. These are the *Feeling of Dependence* and the *Conviction of Moral Obligation.* To these two facts of the inner consciousness may be traced, as to their sources, the two great outward acts by which religion in various forms has been manifested among men ;—*Prayer,* by which they seek to win God's blessing upon the future, and *Expiation,* by which they strive to atone for the offences of the past." Let us suppose for a moment that these data are sound—What is this "Reflection" which acts upon them, and which presumes, as an architect, to build up out of these materials the edifice of Religious Consciousness ? It is a new comer on the philosophical scene. What are its credentials ? How does it differ from the ' philosophy' and the ' speculative reason,' the impotence of which has been so decisively exposed. Mr. Mansel is very strict in exacting from Philosophy demonstrative proof that all she rests upon is above suspicion. He must be governed himself by the law which he has laid down.

The data however are, I venture to submit, very

far from being sound. The word *Dependence* palpably begs the question. We may feel a *weakness*, but to enable us to call that weakness a *dependence*, we must know that there is a Being on whom we depend: and to know this we must form, by our speculative reason, a conception, however imperfect, of a Deity. The weakness of our nature is, to use Mr. Mansel's own phrase, " an immediate fact ;" but the dependence of that weakness upon a Higher Power is not an immediate fact, nor, by the rules of Mr. Mansel's philosophy, can it ever become to us a fact at all.

So, in the phrase *Conviction of Moral Obligation*, the word *obligation* involves a begging of the question. We may be conscious that one faculty in our nature, call it Moral Reason, Conscience, or what you will, predominates over the rest ; but we cannot assume that obedience to this faculty is an *obligation*, without forming a conception of a Being to whom we are bound. This again lets in the speculative reason, and brings the 'edifice' of Mr. Mansel's religious consciousness to the ground. The phrase, 'authority of Conscience,' afterwards used by him, is fallacious in the same way. To convert *power* into *authority*, which is the datum he wants, he must, I apprehend, be cognizant, by speculative reason, of something beyond the power. He must break through his own empiricism, and see, not the "effect" only, but the "cause."

The truth seems to be, as I have above hinted, that Mr. Mansel's "reflection" is, in fact, nothing more or less than speculative reason forming a conception of God.

Besides, supposing the "religious consciousness" to be built up out of these questionable materials by this ambiguous architect, there remains the fatal difficulty stated in a passage of the Bampton Lectures to which I have before adverted. To what "distinct notion" can the "religious consciousness" be referred? If it can be referred to none, it falls under the category of things which cannot be thought of, and which consequently "cannot exist." And it must be remembered that "notions" derived from Revelation will not be available: for Mr. Mansel is here building up a religious consciousness antecedently to Revelation.

When we are told that "the conviction that an Infinite Being exists seems forced upon us by the manifest incompleteness of our finite knowledge," we fall back into the fallacy of the positive-negative *Infinite*. *Infinite* is not the *complement* of *Finite*, but its *negation*. At this rate the philosopher might, by the simple instrumentality of a negative prefix, become the creator of intellectual entities without end. By prefixing a negative particle to *Horse*, he might create the complementary entity *Not-horse* : and then we should have *Not-horse* filling the universe, crushing human reason into the dust and exalting the humility of its enemies to the skies.

When hard pressed by the consequences of his own theory, Mr. Mansel takes refuge in an appeal to *duty*, and tells us (p. 170) that "we are bound to believe that God exists;" forgetting that to be *bound* implies a *Law*, which implies a *Lawgiver*, and so brings us back into the same circle in which we revolved before; the principle upon which our belief in the existence of God depends, depending for its own existence, on our belief in the existence of a God.

When still harder pressed he takes refuge in an appeal to "Faith." In his first lecture he tells us that "Faith (p. 8) properly so called, is not constructive but receptive." Further on in the work, however, I believe it will be found that "Faith" ceases to be merely receptive and becomes constructive in the highest degree. It, in effect, replaces the keystone which the Lecturer has taken out of his own religion, fancying it to be the keystone only of his neighbours.

He "deserts the evidence of reason to rest on Faith"; regulating the measure of Faith, however, so that it may support himself with-

out supporting his opponents, in virtue of some
principle or authority confined to his own bosom,
which enables him to confide in God's representations of Himself as "not totally false," but
does not enable the world at large to confide
in them as entirely true. And yet surely a
mathematician pleading probabilities, the standing
example of intellectual tergiversation, is tolerable
compared with a metaphysican who, having come
into the arena professedly, and amidst great ex-
pectations, to lay philosophy prostrate with her
own weapons, when he finds his position critical,
borrows weapons from faith, and reproaches the
philosopher whom he was to annihilate by demonstration with "parsimony of belief." The object of
the Lectures was to set limits to religious thought;
but faith, in Mr. Mansel's sense, is unlimited;
another man's 'faith' is as good as his : and in
opening the sluice for his own convenience, he
has in fact let in the ocean.

It will be found, I believe, that the "faith"
to which he appeals is in effect a religious obligation antecedent to the existence of a God. At
p. 57 he says "the infinite, as inconceivable, is
necessarily shown to be non-existent; unless we
renounce the claim of reason to supreme authority
in matters of faith, by admitting that it is our
duty to believe what we are altogether unable to

U

comprehend."" Faith must have some object, on the authority of which you accept the proposition in question. What then is the object of this faith which is antecedent to a knowledge of the existence of God? I can really imagine no other than the Oxford pulpit.

The work of M. Bastiat on Economical Sophisms did great service to Economical Science. As great a service would probably be done to Theology by any one who would write an equally good book on Theological Sophisms. The first place among such sophisms would be occupied by *Faith*. There is a reasonable and scriptural Faith which reposes on the Wisdom and Goodness of God, trusts Him entirely, and believes that everything in the ways of His Providence which is now dark will in the end be made clear. But there is also an ecclesiastical faith, neither reasonable nor scriptural, which consists in wilfully shutting the eye of the mind; in putting force upon the conscience; in receiving insufficient evidence and pretending that it is sufficient; in embracing things unworthy of the Deity, and pretending that they are divine. Those who practise this ecclesiastical faith and think it meritorious, tacitly assume that the need of evidence is in an inverse ratio to the importance of the subject; and that while they would be bound to demand full proof before believing that anything of a questionable character came from a good man, they perform an act of piety in believing without full proof, and, sometimes, with no proof at all, that things of a questionable character come from God. The " faith " of the Bampton Lectures is to some extent a new variety of the ecclesiastical species. It is, in fact, a practice of making such metaphysical assumptions as may be requisite to support orthodoxy, while Rational Religion is destroyed. It is employed to fill up, not a defect of evidence, but a void of thought. I fear, however, it rests on the same basis as the other varieties of the same species, and that this basis is something very different from implicit reliance on the God of Truth.

The Deity then remains a ' Negative Idea,' and Religion, of course, remains in a corresponding condition. To Mr. Mansel, indeed, a negative idea seems to be very full of positive significance and comfort. " It is a great mistake" he says " to suppose, as some of my critics have supposed, that if the Infinite, as an object, is inconceivable, therefore the language which denotes it is wholly without meaning, and the corresponding state of mind one of complete quiescence. A negative idea by no means implies a negation of all mental activity. It implies an attempt to think, and a failure in accomplishing the attempt." Religion, according to this account, will be a sort of perpetual effort of the mind to embrace a void—a sort of mental straining after nothing. It is assumed that Man will think it his paramount duty to be always repeating the attempt, notwithstanding innumerable failures, for the sake of the salutary feeling of failure and inanition which results, and that there is no danger of his ever sinking into " quiescence."

Some irreverent Materialists have proclaimed that Theology is an extinct science. The Bampton Lectures reduce it to the science of a negative idea. It will be the duty of the Regius Professor of Theology to expound this negative idea, and to guide the world in straining to apprehend it according to the most orthodox method.

Mr. Mansel, I think, evidently assumes that the negative idea of the Deity has a pre-eminence over all other negative ideas, and is a negative object of reverence, and a negative source of comfort to the soul. But surely the fact is, that one nothing is as good as another nothing ; and that there is no more dignity or comfort in the negative idea of the Deity, than there is in the negative idea of a chimera.

So much for the theory of the matter. But the extent of Mr. Mansel's quotations has unfortunately precluded his noticing my attempt to call his attention to the facts.

That which he metaphysically proves man to be incapable of doing, man has actually done. The mass, even of heathens, have formed for themselves a conception, however gross and imperfect, of the Deity. The higher spirits among them, such as Plato and the great Stoics, formed not only a conception but a very high conception; and the truth of the conception which they formed has been confirmed by an authority which Mr. Mansel will admit to be conclusive. Under these circumstances the question is, whether the philosopher is prepared to say—'So much the worse for the facts.'

He who undertakes to construct a religious philosophy, ought surely in the first place to turn his attention to the facts which make up the history of religion. This neither Mr. Mansel nor Kant has done. Each of them has attempted a sort of a metaphysical operation in a vacuum. Kant shifted the point of inquiry, in effect, from the actual operations of the mind to its capacities, and made it a question not what reason did, but what reason could do: whereby he supposed himself to have affected a most beneficial revolution in philosophy. Mr. Mansel thought that by an adaptation of this process to the special department of Theology, he could summarily strangle reason in its cradle. The result is that he returns,

flushed with victory, from the career of metaphysical destruction, and finds the facts still
confronting him in the field.

The starting point of the Lectures is, I apprehend, the proposition (p. 24) that "the primary
and proper object of criticism is not Religion,
natural or revealed, but the human mind in its
relation to Religion." Let Mr. Mansel compare
this with the doctrine to which he has elsewhere
(p. 143) subscribed. "The perceiving subject alone,
and the perceived object alone, are two unmeaning
elements, which first acquire a significance in and
by the act of their conjunction." If the perceiving
object alone is an unmeaning element, how much
meaning will there be in a criticism of it, or in a
philosophy of which that criticism is the basis?
Where is the use of attempting to determine the
range of a perceptive power, whether it be that of
the eye or of the mind, without reference to the
things which it actually perceives?

Kant compared the revolution effected by him in
speculation to the revolution effected in Astronomy
by Copernicus, when he thought of investigating
the apparent motion of the heavens from the side of
the spectator, instead of from that of the object.
Mr. Mansel applauds the comparison. It would
surely have been an apter one if Copernicus, instead
of investigating the motions of the heavens, had set

to work to investigate the powers of observing such motions possessed by his own eyes.

Man has actually formed for himself an idea of a Deity as an account of his own moral nature, and of the providence visible in the world. This idea, though not strictly universal, is general, and common to the most widely distant and unconnected nations. It grows in purity, in intensity, and in practical influence on the moral life as man rises in the moral scale. No rational account has ever been given of its existence on the supposition that it is not true. Nor has any man yet completely succeeded in reasoning himself out of it. The Positivists have tried hard, and they have ended in a Providence under the name of a "destiny," which they "lovingly accept," a worship of Humanity, and a subjective immortality of the soul. Mr. Herbert Spencer has tried hard, and he has ended, both as a philosopher and a writer on education, in inculcating reverence for "the Unknown." Mr. Mansel has tried harder than any of the rest, in his efforts to destroy the foundation of Rational Religion; but, as we have seen, he has not succeeded in entirely divesting his 'negative idea' of attributes which show that behind it there lurks a conception of God.

The idea of Deity is formed in the human mind, in which and in its instinctive operations, however, we may rationally suppose its Maker to be as present as He is in the rest of the universe. It follows of necessity that the morality contained in the idea must be that which is present in the human mind ; in other words, it must be human morality idealized and personified in God.

The idea is at once perfected and verified by everything that Man, from age to age, learns of himself, and of the world around him, by his scientific discoveries, and still more by his moral experience. But its highest and only complete verification is the Manifestation of the Divine Nature which is recorded in the Gospels, and which, recognized and embraced by the whole Nature of Man, as the diviner part of himself, and the key to the enigma of his being, has transmuted the whole subsequent history of mankind. Revelation might possibly be rendered needless by reason, if it were a set of speculative propositions in theology. It might then be truly said that the " highest praise to which Revelation could aspire was that of coinciding, partially or wholly, with the independent conclusions of Philosophy," and it would follow that " so far as Philosophy extended, Revelation would become superfluous." But Revelation is not a set of propositions in Theology. It is a manifestation of the Divine Nature. It may be said to be superseded by Philosophy only if the longing super-

sedes the fulfilment, if the recognition supersedes
the thing recognized, if the capacity for adoration
supersedes the object which is adored, if the thirst
for the water of life supersedes the fountain from
which that water flows. Does Philosophy supersede
the manifestation of character, and the influence of
veneration and affection, even between man and
man?

Let us only have a little patience. The Philosophy of History is yet young. Philological
criticism is not old. Neither the one nor the other
can pretend, without standing self-convicted of
false pretensions, to have as yet arrived with
certainty at any one important conclusion, of a
positive kind, on the subjects concerning which so
much anxiety prevails. Against any difficulties
that either of them may have raised, is to be set the
fact that Christianity has been for eighteen
centuries, and still is, the life of the world; while
upon its essence, as a manifestation of Divine
Character and a rule of spiritual life, no serious
attack has yet been made. Surely, as regards
secondary questions, we may wait till the historical
and critical problems, now under discussion, have
been solved by the sciences to which they
respectively belong. Reason is the creation of
God; and it is not likely that He will be dethroned
by the work of His own hands. At all events, if

x

the worst is to come, and mankind has been brought suddenly to a dark abyss, no inventions of " two Moralities," no figments of any sort or kind will avert, or even delay the terrible hour.

Mr. Mansel imagines that I was prejudiced against his book by my theory of history; that I condemned him without a fair hearing as an enemy to " progress ;" and that I am raising against him " the cry of Priestcraft," which was raised by " the demagogues of a former generation."

If he will do me the honor to refer to the Lectures of which he is speaking, he will find, in the first place, that the theory of human progress there adopted is identical with the progress of Christianity; and, in the second place, that it recognizes and embraces all honest effort, whether it be made on the side vulgarly called progressive, or on the side vulgarly called retrograde. To no characters in history, according to this theory, would a larger measure of sympathy be due than to those great natures who have struggled for some neglected principle against the tide of adverse times, and sunk in the overwhelming current, while the principle for which they struggled has reached, through their fortitude, a distant shore. When I see any trace of such a spirit, I will do it homage with all my heart. But there is a widely different spirit, the manifest offspring, as it appears to me, of the union between Church and State, which, in its efforts to prevent the advance of truths dangerous to Establishments, has produced the bloodiest and the vilest pages in the annals of mankind. To this spirit I cannot do homage. Mr. Mansel seems to think that it expired with a former generation. I fear that, though quelled by the growth of a higher morality, it has not been extinguished ; that though enfeebled, it has not been softened ; and that whenever an opportunity is afforded, its presence is visible amongst us still. When people have persecuted as much as civilized society will permit them, they fancy that it is their own Christian tolerance which prevents them from persecuting more.

As to " the demagogues of a former generation," if, by that term, Mr. Mansel means those statesmen who took the lead in abolishing the Penal Code, the Roman Catholic disabilities, and the Test and Corporation Acts, I do not decline the association. If he means the French Revolutionists, I think he will find that whenever I speak of that party, either in my Lectures or elsewhere, I show a pretty strong sense of the calamities which they brought upon the world. But while we deplore and condemn the fatal excesses of the French Revolution, it is as well always to bear in mind the source from which that great disaster flowed. It was not a sudden and

unaccountable eruption of evil, but an effect, the
causes of which, political, social, and religious, are
clearly defined in history. To its political and
social causes we have scarcely anything parallel
in this country. Its religious cause was a State
Church, which, deserted by the convictions of the
people, but retaining their outward allegiance, reduced them to hypocrisy, and, at. last, to atheism.
To this we have a parallel in this country. Fortu-
nately it is one of a very mitigated kind ; but, so far
as its influence extends, it is leading English society
the same way.

I should be very sorry to join in any cry against
" priestcraft," because it might seem to be a cry
against the spiritual influence of the clergy, and to
express feelings towards that body the opposite of
those which, if I may presume to say so, I most
deeply and sincerely entertain. The only cry in
which I am ready to join is a cry for freedom of
religious thought, and the entire abolition of all
State interference with the conscience of man in
matters of religion. I think the time for raising
this cry loudly and resolutely has arrived, if the
faith of the people is to be preserved. A system of
State formularies, tempered by casuistry, may have
its advantages in the eyes of super-subtle politicians
or philosophic ecclesiastics, but it is not one by
which the mass of mankind can live. English

statesmen continue to cherish and uphold it. But, though English statesmen are the best and most upright administrators that the world ever saw, there are some things which they do not study; and they are capable of cherishing and upholding, as a guarantee for religious order, that which is in fact a sure source of religious confusion.

I knew, of course, in taking up Mr. Mansel's Lectures, that they were delivered under the pressure of formularies imposed by the State, and that they consequently could not possess the highest value as a free inquiry after truth. But, excepting in this respect, I read them without prejudice or foregone conclusion of any kind. I found in them a learning which is quite above my praise, and an acuteness worthy of the author of Mr. Mansel's previous works. But I found also, clearly enough, that the theory propounded in them, to use the language of its more cautious admirers, was deficient in a " positive" side[1]; or, in plain English, that it left the world without Morality, Truth, or God. I beg leave emphatically to repeat that I say this of the theory alone, and without the slightest reference to its author's personal convictions, which certain passages of his

[1] One religious journal encourages Mr. Calderwood, the author of the work on 'The Infinite,' to undertake the useful task of supplying a "positive" side to Mr. Mansel's philosophy. A curious division of labour!

work show to be entirely unaffected by his theory; or to his personal character, of which, if there were the slightest occasion for alluding to it, I should not fail to speak with proper respect.

At the end of his letter to me, Mr. Mansel, without very positively reasserting the soundness of his doctrines, commends them, in the words of Bishop Browne, to the keeping of Providence. But Providence will not miraculously interpose to prevent premises destructive of religion from leading to their natural conclusions. It has not interposed to prevent the premises furnished by the Bampton Lectures from becoming the foundation stone of a great system of philosophy, utterly opposed to the Lecturer's convictions, or from confirming the tendencies of some who are inclined to think that the crowning triumph of philosophy is the dethronement of God. The only security against the bad consequence of human speculation is discussion; and, as discussion is necessary, it must not be taken as an offence.